BLOW IT UP!

BLOW IT UP!

The Black Student Revolt at San Francisco

State College and the Emergence of Dr. Hayakawa

DIKRAN KARAGUEUZIAN

Gambit, Incorporated

Boston 1971

To my father

CONTENTS

Introduction
by
James Benét

The major significance of the upheaval at San Francisco State College in 1968–69—a significance that has for many been eclipsed by the rising of Dr. S. I. Hayakawa to national celebrity—was that it marked the first serious effort by a group of black students to remold an American college. For those reporters who, like myself, were on the scene, this proved to be a most difficult happening to describe because events quickly developed military form, with secret strategies and plans and careful security measures on all sides. Dikran Karagueuzian's present account, therefore, tells a great deal that was not and could not be reported at the time it happened, and will be of importance and interest even to those who followed the occurrences from day to day as they unfolded.

Briefly to recapitulate, the Black Student Union at the college announced in early November, 1968, that it was on strike and intended to shut the college down "by any means necessary"—a phrase the group apparently picked up from the Black Panthers. Many believed that the strike was in retaliation for the suspension of a militant black instructor, George Murray, at the insistence of Governor Ronald Reagan. But many others, especially at the college itself, quickly saw that the blacks genuinely believed that their efforts of more than a year to organize a Black Studies Department had been deliberately and evilly blocked. White radical students and a few faculty were their allies from the beginning, but most of the campus appeared to be simply concerned and puzzled over the disruptions of classes and noisy parades through buildings. When police were brought in to control the situation, however, and responded by beating and arresting bystanders and demonstrators quite indiscriminately, a majority of students and a large part of the faculty joined the "strike." And in spite of continued massive police action the demonstrations went on—almost daily, except during the Christmas vacation period—until compromise settlements were negotiated with the teachers' union in January and with the black students the next month. It was the longest student campaign in America in modern times, as its black leaders have been proud to proclaim.

The most difficult problem for reporters was to find out from the black students themselves what they really intended. Communication between blacks and whites in America is often difficult enough under ordinary circumstances because of the differences in dialect and cultures. And the leaders of the Black Student Union were trying their best to conceal their intentions from a college administration that they frankly regarded as an enemy, and later on, from the police. They distrusted the press, with some reason, since most press comment was hostile to them, and their press conferences and public statements were devoted mainly to reiterating their formal demands and to scornfully abusing their opponents. The college administration knew a good deal about their thinking, since it had taken the precaution of bugging the supposedly secret meeting at which Stokely Carmichael addressed the black students, and had made a tape recording. But reporters didn't learn of this until later.

Consequently, it was a remarkable journalistic feat for

Dikran to gain the confidence of the intelligent, suspicious black student leaders and to put together from interviews with them the inner story of their campaign. It was the more remarkable, perhaps, since he had been the editor of the student newspaper, the *Gater*, when the strike began. The black students were not overly fond of that paper, which some of them accused of racist remarks, and they had, a year earlier, paid a visit to it which developed into a general fistfight and injury to the editor. (The blacks denied, however, that they went with the intention of beating him up.) Under Dikran's editorship the paper supported the strike editorially. But this was by no means enough to gain a white man their confidence, as this account shows clearly. He was helped by being a Syrian of Armenian descent, so that the blacks considered him a member of a minority—one of the "Third World," as they also described the Asian and Spanish-speaking students who had become recognized allies during the strike. Against that, one must offset that he was talking to them in what is still for him, after all, a foreign language. But somehow he managed it.

Another considerable feat was for a student editor to retain his poise in the midst of the strife and confusion of that time so that he could make a cool decision to resign as editor in order to undertake the more important job of collecting the material for this book. Not that he was aloof from the scene; he had been a busy editor who was on the spot as often as one of his reporters. I used to encounter him on the campus frequently as I did my own chores as a television reporter and, since I doubled as a journalism teacher and he had been my student, we swapped bits of information and comments on events. He was as emotionally involved as anyone; only an individual of nearly inhuman lack of feeling could have been unmoved by seeing the ferocious police retaliation that came down upon the blacks and their supporters after window-breaking demonstrations. But Dikran had already, in spite of his brevity of experience, the characteristic ability of the professional newsman to shake off his own reactions and discuss evidence with an effort at impartiality and fairness. His wry skepticism extended to student theory and tactics as well as to the pronouncements of the administration and the police.

Although his paper was generally in support of the black students' demands and expressed revulsion over the police behavior, Dikran wasn't a supporter of any specific student group or faction. Nor have I ever heard him offer an opinion on the question which divides the nation, whether campus disorder is brought about by such groups as Vice-President Agnew's "effete snobs" or the bored idlers blamed by San Francisco State College President S. I. Hayakawa, or whether it is the product of deeper social malaise. His book provides a great deal of empirical evidence on this subject, no doubt. But Dikran doesn't jump to conclusions easily, and he has the good reporter's ability to say, "I don't know."

His former newspaper fell on hard times after he left. Its principal financial support had come from the student body organization, and the state attorney general's office tied up the student funds during the strike on charges they were being misused. The principal accusation was that the money had been used to buy guns for the black militants—although in fact they never used guns. This charge was based on the fact that one student had taken his paycheck to Reno and bought a pistol with it, an event clearly beyond the control of the student government, as of course the attorney general's office knew perfectly well. But the legal action served to penalize all students, of whatever color, who held student body jobs. Most of them were in fact ardent strike supporters. And it crippled the student newspaper, which grew increasingly hostile to Hayakawa. Later he further hampered it by denying it campus office space. Nevertheless the *Gater* continued to publish—although no longer daily—through 1969–70. But eighteen months after the strike ended many thousands of dollars in student funds were still tied up, and the newly elected student officers were resigned to seeing them wholly consumed by legal and administrative charges before state control was ended.

The campus was quiet, on the whole, and whether this is to be regarded as a success for Dr. Hayakawa's severe measures depends on the viewpoint of the observer. One can say safely that the measures he took have played an important part in causing a large number of courageous and idealistic young Americans to come to despise the major institutions of their country. The black students, especially, have been confirmed and deepened in their radicalism, because they strongly believe that their "strike" was simply one more battle in an ancient struggle for the freedom of their people. In the summer of 1970 the Black Studies Department still survived at the college, after a year filled with friction between it and the administration. But its future was unpredictable, because of Dr. Hayakawa's frequent threats to abolish it. Perhaps its strongest support was the view, widespread in the black community, that establishment of this department was an important pioneer step in obtaining educational equality for blacks, so that it has acquired a symbolic importance.

Historians who come after Dikran will have to assess how big a part the national awareness of the San Francisco State strike played in the black demonstrations that followed at other institutions—most notably Cornell, where an end result was the resignation of university President James Perkins. But there can't be any doubt that it did play some part, and that the new militancy of minority students across the nation has contributed importantly to greater force and sophistication in student activism generally.

The end of the story cannot be foreseen. But those who want to understand what has happened so far will need to read this essential contribution to the history of student activism.

1

A Strike Day

IT WAS PAST NOON ON A CLOUDY DAY. THE LAWN IN FRONT OF
the cafeteria at San Francisco State College was crowded with
students waiting for the scheduled strike rally to begin. Some
questioned people passing out leaflets. Some compared impressions of the previous day's events, which had culminated in a
nonviolent march around the center of the campus. Some,
having been arrested and freed on bail, recounted their experiences in jail. Some discussed the new college president, S. I.
Hayakawa, and his policies in dealing with the student strike,
now twenty-nine days old. It was December 5, 1968, and he
had been in office only eight days. Other students, coming
from all directions, joined the small groups spread out across
the lawn. These newcomers exchanged information from the
outside for news of the latest on-campus developments. Few
students discussed their classes. The fall semester, now two
months old, was already dismissed by many as a loss. During
the previous month, they had come to support the strike for
which no end was in sight.

There were many new faces mingled with the familiar ones
that appeared at all rallies sponsored by leftist organizations.

Activists belonging to various Marxist-oriented groups which rallied under the banner of Students for a Democratic Society had been joined by those who had come to support the strike only after seeing the police club and harass their fellow students. Clashes between police and strikers had polarized the campus when other normally apolitical students sided with conservative California politicians who advocated retaliation against protestors.

The number of scattered students had reached almost one thousand now, and white strike spokesmen, identified by the mass media as leaders, who had gathered near the Speakers' Platform, began to estimate the size of the crowd with satisfaction. Yet they were uncomfortable. It was already 12:30, and the rally had been scheduled to begin at noon. After brief deliberation, a white student wearing an army field jacket left the group and climbed onto the platform. Grabbing the bull horn which lay next to the podium, he pressed the button near the handle and began to speak:

"We're going to show the racist administration that we're winning the struggle. . . ."

The students on the lawn continued their conversations. Like the television cameramen stationed on the roof of the cafeteria, they knew that the white student's words would not affect the day's events. By now it had become clear that the Central Committee of the Black Student Union controlled the strike. The black students were giving all the directives, a privilege which they zealously guarded. Today, the black students had gathered on the lawn in front of Ecumenical House, headquarters of the Campus Christian Ministry, which lies directly opposite the main campus entrance at Nineteenth and Holloway Avenues. By noon nearly three hundred of them stood on the small lawn, waiting for the arrival of supporters from San Francisco's black communities.

Shortly after noon, a gray and blue Greyhound bus pulled to a stop in front of the campus, the air hissing loudly from its brakes. The blacks on the lawn across the street turned to look at the new arrivals trickling off the bus and onto the sidewalk. Although most were middle-aged, there were also some high school students among the seventy-five. This group had come to San Francisco State to support the militant black students whom many whites, including Governor Ronald Reagan, did not believe to be representative of California Negroes. The women arranged their clothes as they stepped to the street; the men stretched their legs, occasionally waving to a familiar face on the lawn. Once off the bus, the teenagers swaggered across Nineteenth Avenue, their elders following close behind. As the first arrivals jumped from the sidewalk over the low stone wall and onto the lawn, they were greeted with cheers and shouts. At the insistence of the black students, established black community leaders had organized this group in hopes that their participation in the strike would have a moderating effect. This new support brought the crowd's number to four hundred.

Standing on the wall which runs around the lawn, Ben Stewart, twenty-three-year-old chairman of the Black Student Union, decided that the group was large enough to execute an impressive march to the rally. Although Stewart was BSU chairman, and had earned his position by loyalty and hard work, he was not the most powerful man in the organization. He had grown up in nearby Oakland and had come to San Francisco State from Lowell High School, San Francisco's most prestigious public high school, where he excelled as a track star. In college, Stewart learned to play the role of the black militant. He customarily wears a frown on his face in public, attempting to project an image of uncompromising toughness. Stewart's short, reluctant, telegraphic sentences and his gruff and overbearing tone often make both him and his interlocutor ill-at-ease. He is short and stocky and holds his head back slightly as he walks. Like other black student militants, Stewart wears sunglasses, even under cloudy skies, and during the strike he often sported a navy blue or khaki green wool cap or a beret.

Stewart is aggressive in his dealings with whites, always remaining aloof and unapproachable. On this occasion, he raised both hands above his head, signaling an end to individual conversations among the crowd. The students and their supporters hushed as Stewart spoke.

"We're going to march on campus in a group," he said. "All Third World people come to the front. We are going to have a rally. If we are attacked, we will defend ourselves. We are going to resist."

What Stewart referred to as an attack was the police's usual rough dispersal of the rally crowd. Resistance would probably amount to no more than rock and bottle throwing, but his choice of words so appealed to the crowd's sense of powerlessness and frustration that he was answered with approving shouts of "Right on!" Then one of Stewart's lieutenants, who was stationed beside him on the two-foot wall, circled his hand over his head, motioning the crowd to move.

Each person inched around to face the campus. No one could take more than one slow step at a time without hitting the heels of those ahead. People on the sidewalk began to walk first, those on the lawn and wall jumping to follow. The four hundred people moved across six-lane Nineteenth Avenue. Monitors at the head of the campus walkway, which opens directly onto the sidewalk, prevented the first arrivals from proceeding. Those gathered together at the head of the path stopped to hear Stewart's brief instructions once again.

"All black, brown, and yellow people get to the front. We want all Third World people out in front. And you John Browns," he said, referring to the white activists in the crowd, "you go down too." By Third World people, Stewart meant those of color. A handful of whites and not more than twenty Chinese and Mexican-Americans were scattered among the crowd. Attention was being given to the composition and arrangement of the marchers because this had been publicized as a Third World group. Now the demonstrators formed lines four and five abreast, fanning out across the fifteen-foot-wide asphalt walkway, and prepared to march down the straight portion of a path that runs two hundred fifty feet between the Administration Building and the Business and Social Sciences and Humanities, Language, and Literature Buildings. The Third World strikers couldn't see their white allies until they turned a bend.

At the head of the line, Stewart quickly looked over his shoulder. As the marchers began to move, striding purposefully down the path, Stewart and others began to chant "On strike," shooting a clenched fist above their heads at each word. "Shut it down." The reflex repeated itself. The festive mood apparent on the Ecumenical House lawn had disappeared. The marchers took on an aggressive air, and smiles and laughter were replaced with tight jaws and determined expressions.

"On strike, shut it down." The chants grew louder, some strikers preferring "On strike, blow it up." A few students in the HLL Building peered curiously from classroom windows as the demonstrators began to encounter book-laden white students scurrying in the opposite direction toward the streetcar stop. Although the white students were glad to be leaving campus, their faces remained expressionless as they stepped aside quickly to make room for the advancing blacks. The head of the march steamrolled forward, picking up speed as it neared the end of the straight path. Strikers were four abreast and shoulder to shoulder, their line stretching almost the entire length of the Ad Building. Those at the front of the march finally reached the bend, and looked over the lawn that covers the entire center of the campus.

At the other end of the lawn, the one thousand white students who had massed at the Speakers' Platform began to cheer. Some ran to meet the approaching blacks. Jubilant at the mood and size of the white crowd, the blacks accelerated their pace and intensified their chants. As the marchers reached the edges of the waiting crowd, their friends parted to form an aisle. The black leaders made their way through the crowd and jumped onto the Speakers' Platform, a redwood structure which, tightly packed, accommodates fifty people. Other blacks took positions at the head of the crowd, close to the platform. Loud chanting continued after the blacks had mounted. Finally the chants subsided and the rally began, in defiance of an administration order forbidding such assemblies. First, various community leaders reaffirmed their support for the strike and vowed to stand with the students until their demands were met. Then Jerry Varnado took the bull horn.

On-campus coordinator of the Black Student Union and the most powerful man in the organization, Varnado stepped to the front of the stand. His hazel eyes glaring, he looked out over his largely white audience.

"Power to the people!" Varnado shouted, calmly waiting for the crowd to shout back in unison.

"Power to the people!"

The Speakers' Platform was so crowded with people taller than Varnado that students at the edges of the crowd could not even see him. He stands about five feet, seven inches tall and is heavyset, though not paunchy. The beginnings of a beard were etched across his full, almost rounded cheeks, and a bristly mustache ran above his upper lip down to the corners of his mouth. Like Stewart, Varnado endeavored to project a stern image both before and throughout the strike. He took great pains not to be caught in public with a smile on his face, only occasionally relaxing enough to laugh with a fellow black student. Son of a Baptist deacon, Varnado was born in Magnolia, a small rural town in Mississippi, where, he says, "there are no classes, everybody is poor." At an early age he went with his family to Alcorn, Mississippi, where his father enrolled as a student at the local college. When he was eleven years old, Varnado's family moved to Jackson, Mississippi. There, at the age of seventeen, he was dismissed from his high school for joining the NAACP. This was as much as he could take.

"I wanted to get out of the South, anyhow," he recalls. "The oppression there was something else."

Varnado saw the United States Air Force as an opportunity to flee, and enlisted in 1962. But he was doubly wrong. He was assigned to Lackland Air Force Base in Texas, where he quickly discovered that he was not destined for a military career, despite the Air Force's offer to send him to school. He recalls that he purposely and consistently made himself a nuisance to his superiors, and recounts one incident in his campaign to get out of the armed forces.

"One day a sergeant ordered me to spend the afternoon painting a few stairs. I painted everything, man. The stairs, the sidewalk, the lawn, everything," he recalls.

After a few months, he was transferred to Vandenburg Air Force Base in Northern California, where he continued his policy of being, in his words, "a general fuck-up," and spent forty-five days in the stockade. The Air Force discharged Varnado in 1963.

He then came to San Francisco State. Like most young Negroes in the early sixties, Varnado held what he now calls "typical Civil Rights views." He believed that racial integration, followed by equal opportunity for all, would solve America's racial crisis. But Varnado, like most of his fellow black students, gradually came to believe that black people should take the offensive in dealing with whites rather than wait to be put on the defensive. Accordingly, he frequently threatened and insulted white administrators and student leaders in words marked by intense contempt.

At a meeting of the student legislature during the fall of 1967, Varnado "demanded" that more money be allocated to the Black Student Union. Striding confidently before a semicircle of fifteen student leaders as he made his case, dressed for the occasion in a dark blue business suit with a single-breasted vest, he looked more like a lawyer than a student militant. After making his presentation, Varnado momentarily turned his back on the group. Each hand grasping a lapel of his suit coat, he gazed at the wall awaiting a rebuttal. James Andrews, former dean of activities and administration representative to the student legislature, said the body would need time to appraise Varnado's request. Varnado, about fifteen feet away from Andrews, wheeled around to face him, and in a few rapid strides was hovering over the dean. Jaws rigid and teeth clenched, Varnado looked down on Andrews and jabbed his forefinger at the dean's face, coming within an inch of the shaken administrator's nose.

"When are you devils going to learn," Varnado hissed in a throaty rage, "that there just ain't no more time!" Andrews, who soon afterward took a position at a junior college because he wished to "be treated like a gentleman," was pale with astonishment and fright. Varnado stepped back, satisfied with the shock his comportment had given the legislators.

To many in the white campus community Varnado seemed arrogant and frightening. Yet it was difficult to tell whether he was bluffing. Within the black campus community he was the leader. His surly manners irritated some and embarrassed others, but he retained control of the Black Student Union, commanding respect and thwarting insurgent forces who objected to his style of leadership. Varnado's words for the strike rally were in keeping with his projected image.

"We've got to put Hayakawa up against the wall!" His voice rose in a crescendo, and he strained to get the last word out.

"Right on!" the crowd answered approvingly.

"We must rip off the slavemaster!"

"Right on!"

In black militant rhetoric the term "rip off" carries many meanings, the most extreme being "to kill violently." Although no one took Varnado's words literally, he stirred the students who were already taut with excitement and anticipation.

"We are going to stand up for our rights. The people from the community have come here to support our demands, even if that means standing up to the pigs." Again he seemed barely to squeeze out the last words, but he emphasized "pigs," waving his hand toward the Administration Building, which houses the president's office. Varnado looked directly into the crowd, and pulled the bull horn a little closer to his mouth.

"We are going to move on that Administration Building!"

"All right!"

"Right on!"

"On strike, shut it down," the chants began. The crowd, which had grown to over two thousand, one-third of the students present on campus on any normal day, turned slowly en masse to face the Administration Building and then began to move.

Meanwhile, Don Scoble, assistant to Acting President S. I. Hayakawa, rose from his cluttered desk two doors down the hall from the president's office. He had brought his lunch from home to avoid walking across campus to the cafeteria during the noon hour. Scoble, a thirty-two-year-old graduate of the institution which now employed him, was going to the basement for tea. He stepped into the deserted hallway, pushing the office door closed behind him. The sound of the banging door echoed up and down the empty corridor as Scoble walked twenty feet to the stairwell. After going down the stairs, he stepped into the concrete-floored basement, glancing briefly at the drab, cream-colored pipes hanging just below the ceiling. Scoble turned the corner at the end of the hall and walked into the staff lounge, a small cubicle gleaming with vending machines. After getting a cup of tea, Scoble retraced his steps to the first-floor corridor. He unlocked the door to Room 105, now a makeshift police command post, which was connected to his office. The room was full of policemen, administrators, and observers from the state capital who were waiting to see the outcome of the rally.

By now, the crowd of marching students had reached the steps of the Ad Building. The blacks, except for the middle-aged community leaders, were in front, their white followers spread across the lawn all the way back to the Speakers' Platform. Police photographers on the rooftops had begun to take pictures. The army helicopter which police used for aerial reconnaissance putt-putted loudly as it circled above the students. So many students were crammed on the stairs that it was impossible to move sideways. As the blacks went up, their chants grew louder. Contending that Acting President Hayakawa was a tool in the hands of conservative California politicians, the students shouted:

"We want the puppet! We want the puppet! We want the puppet!"

The blacks continued up the stairs. With fifteen hundred followers at the foot of the stairs and on the lawn, they swung open the glass doors and burst into the lobby of the Administration Building. It was dark inside and deserted. Their chanting reached a feverish pitch as Varnado veered sharply to his right, leading the black students toward the president's office, thirty feet away.

The students continued to spill into the lobby, filling it to capacity. Some blacks reached into their coats and produced crowbars, sticks, and metal pipes. Four pictures of former college presidents which lined the wall leading to the president's door clattered to the floor, as crowbars shattered their frames and pierced the photographs. Excited by the tinkle of broken glass, other blacks began to pound their fists on the walls. Those who couldn't reach a wall stamped their feet and raised their fists with renewed vigor.

"We want the puppet!" The chants continued within the tightly compressed crowd. The lobby was deluged with the noise of insistent shouts and fists thudding against the walls.

"Get that motherfucker out here!" one student shouted.

"Yeah," rejoined another. "Come out, you son-of-a-bitch!"

"If you don't come out, we'll come in after you!" yelled another.

The blacks advanced on the president's office, thumping their pipes and crowbars against the walls. Then Varnado and others began to bang on the president's door, demanding that he come out. While the surging crowd was echoing this ultimatum, students at the door of the building were still attempting to squeeze into the lobby.

Inside the police room, a Sacramento detective rushed through the door which led into the president's outer office. Without knocking, he opened the president's door, showed his identification, and grabbed the acting president's elbow, leading him into his private bathroom.

"I think you'll be safer here, Dr. Hayakawa," he said. Then he told the president's public relations officer, Harvey Yorke, to grab some heavy object for self-defense. Recounting the episode later, Yorke said, "I thought to myself, 'Drop dead!' "

Administrative Assistant Scoble remembers, "We didn't know exactly what was happening." After a few minutes of confusion, the six San Francisco policemen assigned to the Administration Building emerged from the police room, and moved swiftly toward the head of the crowd, now pressed against the president's door. No students moved to resist the advancing police. Ordering the students to move back, they wedged their way between the shouting blacks and the office door. Barely moving enough to allow the police to guard the door, the blacks continued to chant. For thirty seconds it was a standoff, the police almost chin-to-chin with the angry strikers. Overcoming his initial shock, a black student at the front of the crowd reached into his jacket pocket, ducked slightly as he drew out a can of Mace, and sprayed in the officers' direction. Like insect repellent, the mist hissed forth from the container, dotting the officers' visors but not reaching their eyes. Immediately, two officers pulled their guns and waved them menacingly at the crowd. Then two other policemen drew their Mace and sprayed point-blank.

At the sight of drawn guns, many strikers madly attempted

to scatter, but the lobby was so crowded that escape was difficult. Pushing and shoving, they attempted to get out of the building. Seeing their frantic efforts to escape, those on the outside of the building also tried to retreat. Some students in the rear of the lobby rushed out the back hallway. Meanwhile, the grim-faced police officers held their ground, two still pointing their guns as the last students fled the building.

Minutes later a policeman stepped into the police office gingerly holding a partially opened attaché case. As he moved into the room, another policeman in the office warned, "There's a bomb inside!" A .45-caliber revolver, cocked and loaded, and a transistorized device which looked like a homemade bomb were partially visible inside the case. At that point, Scoble recalls, he "thought it prudent to leave the room." The administrative assistant moved through the chain of interconnecting offices into the president's waiting room. As he entered, Scoble met Hayakawa, who was in his shirtsleeves, heading for police headquarters.

"You'd better not go in there, sir," Scoble warned, grabbing the acting president's arm, "there's a bomb in that room."

Unperturbed, and without a word to anyone, Hayakawa turned back into his private office, while his secretary, at the thought of a bomb two doors down the hall, nervously began to rearrange the flowers which the acting president had received from well-wishers.

Outside the office, police sealed the doors to the building to prevent another assault. The students who had invaded the lobby had retreated to the outside stairs, their followers regrouped on the ground beneath them. Encouraged by the relative success of the initial siege—they had come within yards of Hayakawa and had forced the police to draw their guns—the leaders were urging students to stage a new assault. Jerry Varnado seized the bull horn from another black student who was informing the crowd, "The pigs drew their guns to shoot the people."

"We've got to go in and fight the pigs!" Varnado exclaimed. Then he handed the bull horn to a fellow black student. The listening students seemed confused. They appeared reluctant to act upon Varnado's words. Yet he readied himself "to fight the pigs" by hurriedly smearing Vaseline on his face in anticipation of another Mace attack. For a moment, it looked as if he were going to re-enter the building alone.

In the pandemonium, even amplified voices went unheard. The students ignored the speakers' exhortations, and looked around warily for the police. Tactically, the crowd was in a poor position. It was surrounded on three sides, by the Ad Building, the Business and Social Sciences Building, and the Library. The only road clear was back toward the Speakers' Platform. An anonymous voice rose above the din:

"Let's move on BSS!"

Other voices shouted approval. The BSS Building, located at the rear of the crowd, opened onto the central campus area and offered a better position. The march leaders now began to file down the steps, their followers moving back to give them room.

With the steps clearing, some strikers reached into their pockets for objects ranging from bricks to pine cones. They hurled these missiles at the windows of the president's conference room. As they hit their mark sporadically, the breaking glass aroused whoops and yells among the strikers' chants.

Following this short barrage, the strikers turned to march on the BSS Building, which had become a symbol of campus conservatism. It houses the History and Business Departments, whose students and faculty had, for the most part, strongly condemned the strikers and their goals. The leaders of the march moved up the path along the side of the building. Approaching the entrance, they slowed their pace, turned to face the doors, and began to shake their fists. The line of strikers then started to snake through the trees in front of the building, chanting, "On strike, shut it down!" As they massed along the path and in the clearing in front of the building, rocks began to fly with more frequency, and the sound of breaking glass was heard again and again. Some students, embarrassed by the window smashing, drowned their discomfort with louder chants. Others turned away, but were unable to escape the sounds of shattering glass and subsequent yells of satisfaction. One student lamented, "This is just what they want us to do." He was answered only by those who felt that rock throwing wasn't enough.

"Blow the motherfucker up!"

As the whoops got louder and the rocks flew faster, a group of five students seized a metal garbage can at the foot of the short staircase leading to the main door of the building. Banging on the can, they stirred the crowd's frenzy further. When their drumming had reached an ear-shattering pitch, they lifted the can, two on each side and one in the rear. Starting a few feet from the foot of the steps, they began to run up toward the double doors. Quickly scaling the stairs, they drew the garbage can back and, from a distance of two yards, hurled it full force at the glass door.

The metal can barreled through the door with a resounding crash. The crunch and tinkle of broken glass momentarily halted the shouting, as the militants, exhilarated by their daring act, disappeared into the crowd. The rest of the students, who had formed a rough line facing the building, gave no sign of reducing their attack. Eventually, a line of San Francisco police marched around one side of the building toward the students, approaching them along the path. Seeing the police, the students retreated into the open area between the BSS Building and the center of campus. As they moved back in all directions, a line of thirty policemen cordoned off the building.

At the rear of the crowd, a small group of black community leaders, who had been watching the action from afar, with the hope of preventing violence urged the withdrawing students to march with them to the Speakers' Platform for another rally. Two thousand strikers now massed in confusion in the center of the campus lawn while police arrived from their stations on nearby streets as far as half a mile away. The officers who had secured the BSS Building remained in position. Five other flanks of police, each composed of about seventy-five officers, moved into place, to form a hexagon surrounding the crowd. One line of police stood ready on the path in front of the Library, which stands next to the Ad Building. Another flank formed in front of the cafeteria, usually called the Commons. Still another emerged from the Men's Gymnasium, a favorite police stronghold, and took its position in front of the Speakers' Platform, to wall off the podium toward which the black community leaders were preparing to lead the strikers.

Just as the demonstrators were gathering near the trees in front of the BSS Building, Acting President Hayakawa spoke over the public address system loaned to the college by the California Disaster Corps. Dubbed "Big Brother" by the students, the unit emanated sound which could be heard over a five-mile radius.

"This is your acting president," Hayakawa began.

"Fascist pig," some students responded.

"I order you to clear the campus immediately. I repeat, I order you to disperse." Hayakawa's normally childlike voice boomed.

"Leave the campus at once. There are no longer any innocent bystanders," he went on. At this, many who had been watching the demonstration from the lawn began to join the catcalls.

"Clear the campus. I thought if you talked you would quiet down and go away. But things are escalating now. I don't want anyone to get hurt." These final statements by the acting president were met with laughter and increasing profanity.

"Fuck you," somebody yelled.

The black community leaders, although shaken by this massive show of police force, began to march toward the Speakers' Platform and the line of police guarding it. Only about five hundred students followed them. The rest quietly crossed the police lines or remained on the lawn away from those who chose to march.

The marchers were led by Dr. Carlton Goodlett, a physician and publisher of a successful Negro weekly, who had been hoisted onto the shoulders of his followers. Swaying somewhat precariously, a bull horn in his hand, he led the crowd directly toward the police unit in front of the platform. As the group moved past the clump of trees, a line of police about thirty yards away came forward. Dr. Goodlett, visibly frightened, raised his hand above his head and shouted:

"We're not subscribing to violence at this time. If the police feel that doing their duty involves physical violence then all hell is going to break loose."

As his group approached the wall of policemen, Dr. Goodlett continued his explanations. Finally, with only five feet separating the two groups, he told the police that they could make arrests, but not "persecute people." Lieutenant James Curran, the officer in charge of the San Francisco Tactical Squad, a group of forty officers supposedly trained for riots, retorted with an order to disperse. When the crowd didn't comply, the police charged.

The students attempted to run. Those who weren't fast enough were clubbed or shoved by cursing police officers. White-coated medics and nurses, moving toward fallen demonstrators, were repelled by police who prodded them with thirty-inch riot nightsticks. A previously alerted paddy wagon, traveling at high speed, arrived amid the cheering remarks of some fifty San Francisco State athletes and other supporters of the acting president who could be identified by their blue arm bands. Some of these hecklers gleefully invited police to assault the demonstrators further, "to kill them." Although Goodlett showed no intention of resisting, the sergeant in charge automatically grabbed his left arm and twisted it behind his back. But almost immediately, he released it in embarrassment, and led the black physician to the paddy wagon. Dr. Goodlett was booked at the City Jail on charges of failure to disperse, unlawful assembly, disturbing the peace, and violation of the Mulford Act, a California ordinance prohibiting unauthorized nonstudents from entering a California State College or University.

Meanwhile, other flanks of policemen had moved in on Dr. Goodlett's supporters. Two white clergymen were arrested without violence, but students often received rough treatment. Now a contingent of one police flank was moving toward the remnants of the crowd, ordering people to leave. Catching stragglers, and occasionally clubbing them, the police made further arrests. The ring of police continued to tighten around the demonstrators. Since most of the students were now on the outskirts of the central campus area, police began to make a wide sweep to force them off campus. The demonstrators began to flee, the largest group, nearly one thousand in number, retreating along the main campus path the blacks had used to begin their march. The police followed, arresting students indiscriminately and clubbing the rear guard of strikers who were unable to move fast enough to get away. The students filed onto Nineteenth Avenue. After police chased the last of them from the campus, the main walkway was sealed off.

An uneasy calm pervaded the grounds. Police formed cordons at all entrances to the BSS and Administration Buildings, and would not allow anyone into the Library. Other squads of police lined the narrow passageways between various campus buildings. No students were allowed to cross police lines, either to enter or leave buildings. Some were lined up against the walls and frisked. No one was allowed to move freely. Insults and obscenities from off campus could still be heard occasionally and the officers peered nervously in the direction of this anonymous insolence. Secretaries who had left their offices moved to the windows in the halls and stood watching, some with their arms folded across their chests, frightened and unsure of what would follow. Students left in the HLL Building stood at the windows craning their necks to catch a glimpse of the confusion at the main entrance to the campus.

The first students to arrive at the intersection of Nineteenth and Holloway Avenues crossed immediately, disregarding street lights, and hundreds more began to follow. An irate motorist, driving up Nineteenth Avenue and determined to cross the intersection, screeched to a halt only a few inches from a student in the crosswalk.

"Watch where you're going," an enraged student bellowed.

The driver kept quiet, but fumed behind the wheel as even more students poured into the street. Soon the white lines of the crosswalk could no longer be seen as the strikers spilled over its borders. Most of the demonstrators moved through the intersection toward their cars, which were parked on residential streets nearby. But nearly five hundred remained behind, some only curious, others still intending to confront the police. With groups of students still milling about in the intersection and watching from sidewalks and the Ecumenical House lawn, traffic was completely halted. Some motorists were trapped in the intersection, and the line of autos reached back for blocks on both sides of Nineteenth Avenue. Amid the commotion, a Municipal Railway streetcar pressed through the crowd. With only a few yards to go to clear the intersection, the vehicle was stopped by four students who walked in front of it and stood on the tracks. Two other students ran to the rear of the car and yanked the electric cable, pulling it from the trolley wire and leaving twenty feet of the streetcar jutting into the intersection. Then they casually moved on.

Encouraged by this act, other demonstrators overturned aluminum trashcans, setting fire to piles of garbage, and hurled newspaper vending racks into the street. The most remarkable of this series of spontaneous deeds of vandalism occurred when six students decided to damage parked cars. Their indiscriminate attacks were halted when a black student told them:

"Don't do that. These are people's cars. This way there's a pig's car. Let's get the damn thing into the street and mess up Holloway." By "people," he meant either students or strike sympathizers. Everyone else was a "pig."

The militants, welcoming direction, agreed, and the black student led them to a station wagon parked between two other cars on Holloway Avenue, facing downhill toward the chaotic intersection. They surrounded the car, which belonged to United Press International. After smashing the driver's window, the black student released the hand brake and put the car in neutral. Then he ordered his comrades to help roll it into the street and down into the intersection.

While these students were busy, a line of California Highway Patrolmen marched onto the street to clear the intersection. Noticing the police some fifty yards away, the black student yelled: "The pigs are coming. Let's get it into the street!"

With a final push, they had the station wagon rolling slowly. As the car came toward them, the police officers broke ranks and ran after the demonstrators who were fleeing up Holloway. Three of the slower students were caught. The police beat one of them who had fallen, severely fractured the skull of the second, and gave the third a deep gash on the back of his head.

When the station wagon had gone a few yards down the hill, it bumped into the cement island in the middle of the street and came to a stop undamaged. As students fled, they discharged their surplus ammunition by lobbing it at the police who were advancing nearly one hundred yards away down the hill. After the police ceased their pursuit, the students, now only about seventy-five in number, continued up Holloway toward Junipero Serra Boulevard. Their attempts to stall traffic at this intersection failed.

The angry driver of one of the first cars to escape the Nineteenth Avenue jam entered the intersection, making a left turn onto Junipero Serra without reducing his speed. His gray English sports car grazed a black student who was crossing the street. Distraught at the sight of a fallen black student, the driver slowed down. But when the students ran angrily toward his car, he sped away. A few ran after it, one of them hurling a rock, which shattered the passenger window.

By three-thirty in the afternoon, most of the two thousand demonstrators had gone, leaving behind them leaflets, picket signs, and missiles littering a quiet campus and several hundred policemen guarding the buildings and the college entrances against another march. Most classes had been canceled, despite administration assertions to the contrary. Those professors who taught did so because they were determined to carry on, if even a few students showed up. Some had met their scheduled classes not so much because they wanted to express their disapproval of the strikers and their goals as because they felt they had a moral obligation both to teach and to stay above campus politics. Those who felt that strike conditions were an impediment to learning had chosen to teach off campus, either in their homes or in the halls of neighborhood churches. Faculty members who sympathized privately with the strikers outnumbered the one hundred who honored student picket lines. Those who refused to teach spent their scheduled class time either talking with students or attending their mass meeting in hopes of ending the crisis.

The striking students considered December 5 a victory. Their purpose had been to halt the college's normal operations until their demands were met, and they felt that they had succeeded in doing so. It was with slogans like "We won again!" that they had left the campus. But Acting President Hayakawa and his supporters also claimed victory merely by having it on record that San Francisco State had remained officially open on this day. It mattered little to them that this was achieved with the assistance of six hundred police officers who included members of the California Highway Patrol and policemen who came from cities as far away as Dixon, seventy miles north of San Francisco.

Hayakawa's predecessor, Robert Smith, had closed the college down in attempts to end the crisis, angering the governor, the trustees, and many members of the state legislature, who had publicly chastized him for "giving in to the radicals." The new president was determined "to keep the campus open" at any cost, and from Sacramento the governor had said, "He's our man; he's doing a good job."

On this day, twenty persons had been arrested and many injured. State property had been damaged. Acting President Hayakawa had given the San Francisco Police Department a free hand to reinforce his emergency rules forbidding mass assemblies and the use of equipment to amplify sound. The crisis had begun on October 28, when a Black Panther at San Francisco State announced a list of grievances which centered on the Black Studies Department and the admission of black students to the college. On November 4, at a highly publicized and eagerly awaited press conference, the black students had made public ten "nonnegotiable" demands for which they would strike.

Their demands were:

1. That all Black Studies courses being taught through various other departments be immediately part of the Black Studies Department and that all the instructors in this department receive full-time pay.
2. That Dr. Hare, Chairman of the Black Studies Department, receive a full professorship and a comparable salary according to his qualifications.
3. That there be a Department of Black Studies which will grant a Bachelor's Degree in Black Studies; that the Black Studies Department Chairman, faculty and staff have the sole power to hire and fire without the interference of the racist administration and the Chancellor.
4. That all unused slots for Black students from Fall 1968 under the Special Admissions Program be filled in Spring 1969.

5. That all Black students who wish to, be admitted in Fall 1969.
6. That twenty (20) full-time teaching positions be allocated to the Department of Black Studies.
7. That Dr. Helen Bedesem be replaced in the position of of Financial Aid Officer and that a Black person be hired to direct it and that Third World people have the power to determine how it will be administered.
8. That no disciplinary action will be administered in any way to any students, workers, teachers, or administrators during and after the strike as a consequence of their participation in the strike.
9. That the California State College Trustees not be allowed to dissolve any Black programs on or off the San Francisco State College campus.
10. That George Murray maintain his teaching position on this campus for the 1968–69 academic year.

2

Revolution Has Come

ON MONDAY MORNING, OCTOBER 28, JERRY VARNADO, ON-campus coordinator of the Black Student Union, arrived at Faculty Parking Lot Number Seven a few minutes before ten o'clock. After parking his immaculate '65 Ford, he took his briefcase and began to walk slowly toward the BSU office. He still had a few minutes before his 10:10 class, and he wanted to spend them there. Looking straight ahead, with an angry expression on his face, he walked slowly past the Art Building. It was still chilly, and the narrow paths that run between the lawns were wet from the thick, early-morning fog that covers the southwestern parts of San Francisco almost every day. As Varnado approached the office, students began coming out of their classes and going toward the cafeteria. Of those who recognized him, some attempted to look at him inconspicuously, while others continued on their way, pretending they had not even noticed him. Varnado walked on, his head up, his frown unrelenting. In the office, a young girl greeted him with a smile, but Varnado's reply was inaudible. He strove for a uniform image, rather than reserving his aloofness for whites.

The waiting room of the BSU office was decorated with pictures of Stokely Carmichael, Huey Newton, and other contemporary blacks who are popular spokesmen for black youth. Next to the pictures was a bulletin board for messages. Not finding anything for him, Varnado entered the adjacent office, where he always discouraged the presence of others, preferring to be alone. As soon as he had sat down, the girl in the outer office, who—like many other BSU "sisters"—served as a part-time secretary, timidly reminded him that since it was near the end of the month he should sign the authorizations for student workers' salaries. At the beginning of the year at San Francisco State, after having been allotted a certain amount by the Associated Students, who had an annual working budget of close to four hundred thousand dollars, each student organization was free to spend the money as it pleased. Two officers were responsible for its finances, and only with their signatures could money be paid out. For the most part, the allocated money was used for salaries. "I haven't forgotten," Varnado said calmly and confidently, "I'll sign them after class."

By now it was past ten, and Varnado went to his class, which was composed mainly of black students, some of them special admittees. Like other BSU leaders, Varnado taught a class while attending school himself. These teaching positions had been obtained through the efforts of professors who believed that rules for hiring such teachers should be relaxed in the case of black students. That semester, three weeks after school had begun, the Social Science Department had agreed to open a new section of Soc Sci 30 and had offered Varnado a job teaching this general education course in economics. His section was intended especially for black students and was to be incorporated into a Black Studies curriculum when it came into being. Varnado once said that the students in his economics class were surprised to see a teacher like him who, although very formal, treated them as equals. As a result of the example he had set, his students had begun to require similar treatment from their other professors, Varnado said, adding that his students were excited at finding out that such a student-teacher relationship could exist. For Varnado, student-teacher relationships had changed at State over the past few years. He attributed this change to the growing influence of the Black Student Union in campus affairs.

Shortly before eleven o'clock, Varnado dismissed his class and, accompanied by three of his students, returned to the BSU office, which by now had become noisier, as black students went in and out. The office provided many of the services one would normally expect from the office of the dean of students, which the new black students feared. At the BSU office, black students were offered advice and guidance. New students who were at a loss to cope with all the IBM cards and registration forms they had received could find out exactly what was expected of them. Names of professors who sympathized with blacks were also available, and students who had poor grades were given the titles of easy courses.

Making his way through the crowd in the waiting room, Varnado entered his office. A picture of Kathleen Cleaver hung on the wall next to his desk. As he began to sign the authorizations, he reviewed the entire BSU budget to determine how much money was left. At the rate the organization was spending its more than twenty-thousand-dollar allotment, soon there would be no money left, but he decided he'd worry about that when it happened.

Shortly after 11:30, a tall black man walked into the BSU office, wearing dark sunglasses and a black leather jacket. He was accompanied by six others in similar garb. Varnado, recognizing "D. C.," Field Marshal of the Black Panther Party, stood up and greeted him with a smile. For a moment, everyone in the office interrupted their talk to look at Donald Cox. BSU Chairman Benny Stewart, who was in one of the three adjacent offices, came out to learn what had caused the sudden quiet. During this period, both Varnado and Stewart often hinted publicly at their close ties with the Panthers, particularly after rumors that they had differed with members of that organization. As a matter of fact, after reaching national prominence, the Panthers did not show much interest in the BSU except that earlier that year D. C. had temporarily sat on the Central Committee upon the insistence of the students. But the BSU leaders encouraged, by their silence, rumors associating them with the Panthers, whose advice they occasionally solicited.

Now the excitement at the presence of a top Panther official subsided and conversations were resumed. D. C. asked Varnado and Stewart how things were going and what they were doing that day.

It was a year earlier on this day that Huey P. Newton was involved in the shoot-out with Oakland police which resulted in one officer's death. Stewart and Varnado spoke of "Huey," as his admirers refer to him, with love and respect, and D. C. seemed pleased. As they were exchanging pleasant memories of Huey, who on the day of the shoot-out had talked to a group of students at San Francisco State, another Panther official walked into the office. George Murray, also a student and part-time teacher like Varnado, greeted them and, grabbing a chair from an office next door, joined the group. Although Murray kept close, friendly ties with Varnado and other BSU leaders, since becoming a Panther he no longer associated himself with the student organization. Murray is about Varnado's age and comes from the same rural area in Mississippi, some sixty miles from Varnado's home town. He too had a religious upbringing. His father is a minister in the Presbyterian Church. Their similar backgrounds had made the two closer to each other than to the friends they had in common. Like Varnado, Murray had been a civil rightist before he became a black militant advocating armed revolution. In 1963, the year he came to San Francisco, Murray had worn a Quo Vadis or close-cropped haircut and had often appeared in a royal blue, single-breasted blazer and tie. Now he wore a bushy natural and a three-quarter-length black leather jacket, the Black Panther Party uniform.

Murray had just finished teaching an English class in the HLL Building, and said he had dropped by to see "what was happening." Outside, a tape recorder was playing a speech by Stokely Carmichael, and the crowd of students—both black and white—was growing. The sky was still uniformly gray, with no indication that the sun would appear that day. Every now and then, a passing student slowed down his pace to determine the nature of the speech or guess the identity of the speaker. That semester, the BSU had begun to play taped speeches and soul music in front of their office around noon, and the sound could always be heard within a radius of fifteen to twenty yards, sometimes even farther. About twelve o'clock, D. C. and his six companions left the BSU office, and went to the cafeteria across the path.

As Stewart, Varnado, and Murray stood in front of the door after the Panthers had left, Murray became very serious. Leaning his head slightly to his right, and making circular motions with his index finger, he told Stewart and Varnado, "I think we should have a demonstration for Huey today. He'd lay down his life for the people, and we should honor him." Varnado and Stewart agreed with him, and summoned the black students standing near the office to tell them about the plan. These students, in turn, went to the cafeteria and the areas surrounding it to notify other black students of the commemoration. By now it was past twelve, and other students were heading toward the cafeteria from their eleven o'clock classes. As the number of black students on the path between the BSU office and the southern wing of the Commons Building swelled to over one hundred, many white students who had gathered in the vicinity to eat lunch looked on curiously. Occasionally, a white student on the periphery of the crowd would ask someone he recognized about the reason for the assembly, without getting any reply. In the presence of other members of their own race, many black students would not talk to a white, particularly on such an occasion as this, when the mood was angry. Black students who were arriving now joined the group, after they had learned of the plan to march around campus. Remembering this day, Varnado says proudly that when the black students wanted to gather their "brothers," they could do so in a matter of minutes. Whenever such a summons is sent out from BSU Headquarters, black students respond immediately. On one occasion, Varnado and other black leaders, finding themselves surrounded by close to thirty physical education students at a meeting of the Student Legislature, and feeling threatened, sent out word that their lives were in danger. Within the space of five minutes, the thirty white athletes had been matched by an equal number of militant blacks.

Now the tapes and conversations were halted, and Benny Stewart told the gathered blacks that they would march around campus to commemorate Huey's arrest. Angry shouts of "Free Huey" rang out, followed by even angrier responses, "Free Huey."

Frowning, Stewart made his way through the crowd and began the march toward the cafeteria. The other blacks followed behind him quickly in twos and threes, forming a long line. In quick steps, Stewart marched up to the Redwood Room of the Commons, and angrily threw open the doors, leading the group through the congested hall. There, where numerous vending machines carry everything from cigarettes to hot, greasy pastrami sandwiches, students too poor to buy meals in the cafeteria eat their lunch.

Raising a clenched fist, Stewart chanted, "Black is Beautiful," to which the group responded, "Free Huey." Those in the front lines accompanied Stewart as he repeated the same cry, this time getting a louder reply. Stewart and his companions then chanted, "Set our warrior free," and the crowd responded, "Free Huey." All activity in the Redwood Room was suddenly halted at the sight of almost two hundred black students, or—

as some thought of them—BSU members. Seeing everyone's attention directed toward them, the blacks made their chants louder and shook their fists with more force.

Stewart now led his followers through the International Room or cafeteria, where all movement froze for the duration of the blacks' march, as they moved through the room and out the main entrance of the cafeteria. Then they began to march toward the Administration Building, which by now had become a symbol to them of everything evil at San Francisco State. Although Stewart hadn't originally intended to march through the Administration Building, as he stepped out of the cafeteria, he decided that this was a good opportunity to make a show of force, particularly when so many blacks had gathered en masse. Not everyone in his group was a registered student. Some were young Panther Party members from the city's ghettos, frequently at San Francisco State to be with their friends, most of whom were special admittees. Other blacks did not belong to any organization and came to the college simply for lack of anything better to do. Many had made a habit of spending their days around the BSU office or with BSU members who enjoyed considerable prestige on campus.

Since it was lunch hour, the administration offices were officially closed, and the halls of the building were deserted. Occasionally a secretary would come out of a locked office to go into the restroom. Without incident, the blacks filed through the Ad Building with mischevious smiles on their faces, and left. Now the chant was "Revolution has come"; the response, "Off the pig."

"Time to pick up the gun."

"Off the pig."

As the march moved through the center of campus, Stewart turned around to face the line and, walking backward, signaled to the crowd to chant louder. He raised both hands angrily, shouting "Revolution has come," with all his might, to which the crowd responded "Off the pig." Satisfied, Stewart turned around and continued to lead the marchers back to the cafeteria.

Once inside, the blacks marched through the aisles to the southwest corner of the large room, which had recently been painted a dull, reddish brown. Letters had been addressed to the student daily paper accusing the cafeteria management of choosing this color to discourage students from spending their time there. As one enters, the far left side of the International Room is unofficially the black students' corner, just as the northwest section is the Arab and Iranian students'. In the blacks' section, the black students who constituted the college's black bourgeoisie were eating lunch, unconcerned about the march. They still preferred to be called Negroes.

Within seconds, the blacks had brought a few tables together and swept the dirty dishes to the floor, creating a platform for their speakers. Students sitting at the nearby tables, startled, looked in the direction of the falling dishes. Benny Stewart immediately jumped atop the tables to tell the puzzled crowd who had been eating that the blacks were commemorating their Black Panther leader, Huey P. Newton, on the anniversary of his arrest. As Stewart was explaining that Newton was the victim of institutionalized racism, he noticed George Murray, who had just walked into the cafeteria. Murray had been sitting outside the BSU office while his friends marched. Believing that Murray was a better public speaker than he, Stewart now shortened his remarks, and—to Murray's surprise—announced his name as the next speaker.

Murray, the Black Panther Minister of Education, was a well-known figure in California, and conservative California politicians often used him as an example of what was wrong with higher education. Earlier in the month, under pressure from these politicians, the trustees had raised doubts about the suitability of having Murray teach classes at San Francisco State. A controversy had arisen the previous year, when Murray was identified as one of the assailants of Jim Vazcko. Vazcko was the student editor of the *Daily Gater* at that time, and the publication was under the authority of the Department of Journalism. After the court put Murray on probation without sentencing him to jail, a faculty investigating committee turned in a report that praised him as an instructor. Then the controversy was revived during the summer of 1968, after Murray gave speeches in Havana, Cuba, wherein he was reported to have favored a Viet Cong victory. Faced with the delicate task of removing Murray without arousing sympathy for him, the Administration decided that it was to be done by due process.

Robert Smith, who was then president of the college, had promised Murray earlier in the month that he would stand by him even if the conservatives in the state tried to have him fired, hoping that his commitment to defend Murray would make the Black Panther instructor more careful about making inflammatory statements in public. In Fresno, Murray had likened the American flag to toilet paper, saying it should be flushed down the toilet—and, on his own campus during a speech against military recruiting, had pointed out the necessity for political assassinations to rid the country of people like Max Rafferty, Ronald Reagan, and even Smith himself.

Today, as Murray stood on the table talking, Smith was having lunch in one of the nearby restaurants, without suspecting that Mr. George Mason Murray, as he often referred to the black instructor, would force him into another controversy with conservative politicians. Meanwhile, the crowd welcomed the young black instructor with cheerful applause, for he was a local hero to many in the audience. Murray successfully projected an image of fierceness. As Varnado was to say later, "Whenever we really wanted to scare somebody, we took George with us." At one meeting with administrators and black students, Murray, grinding his teeth and glaring at an administrator who had the same name as President Smith, said, "Listen, you Motherfucker Smith, we know you're lying. . . ." As his involvement with the Black Panther Party had grown, Murray had come to see himself as more of an ideological leader, and refused to concern himself with petty quarrels at the college. When asked what he thought of the investigation, he would say, "I don't care. It's irrelevant to what we black people are going to do. We're going to keep doing whatever we have to do for black folks." Murray's reaction in private was the same, Varnado recalls. "Whenever I showed him an article in the paper and told him, 'Look at what the pigs have to say about you,' he'd look at it and laugh fiercely. And then we'd all laugh together."

After Stewart had introduced him, Murray told the students listening to him in the cafeteria that the number of black students at San Francisco State had decreased considerably over the past ten years and that efforts to establish a Black Studies Department were failing because of the Administration's reluctance to act.

"The Black Studies Department is no department at all," he said, referring to a newspaper announcement in which the college president had been quoted as saying that there was, in fact, such a department at San Francisco State.

"There are four and one-half million black and brown people in California and they all pay taxes to pay for the racist departments here, but none of their taxes go to black and brown people.

"There are no full-time jobs for the brothers and sisters on the faculty here.

"The crackers still say they have the right to say how many black and brown people will come into this school and how many will not. There are four and one-half million black and brown people in California, so there should be five thousand black and brown people at this school," Murray asserted.

"It's just the same as in the communities where the crackers make black people wage slaves," he went on, with a gesture characteristic of him in public speaking, moving his hands, held in front of his chest, in swift circles away from his body.

Murray attributed the decrease in the percentage of black

students at San Francisco State to the racist policies of the
state of California. But, in fact, the decline had occurred in recent years because the Master Plan for Higher Education,
which had gone into effect, shunted off students with lower
grades to junior colleges. In the early sixties, black students at
State had made up approximately eleven percent of the student body. In the fall of '68, they accounted for less than four
percent. As further evidence of racism, Murray now cited the
fact that Nathan Hare, who had been hired eight months before to head the proposed Black Studies Department, received
only $11,550 instead of $18,000, the standard salary of white
department chairmen. Actually, according to administration
policy, professors receive salaries based on academic rank rather
than administrative positions. The conflict was to be verbalized
later.

In an effort to promote the party, Murray defended its policy
of self-defense and suggested that his people "bring guns on
campus to defend themselves against racist administrators." He
also cautioned black students against becoming involved in the
black liberation movement mainly for prestige, telling them it
meant work. While he was talking about social responsibility
and usefulness, he said, he wanted to make clear that Negro
fraternities and sororities had no use. They would become
meaningful only if they "picked up the gun" like the Panthers
and "laid their bodies on the line." Murray had personal reasons for discrediting black social organizations modeled after
white fraternities and sororities. In the mid-sixties, he had
fallen in love with a middle-class sorority girl, and he hadn't
forgotten their conflicts.

"If a fraternity takes up guns to defend our communities
from the pigs, then it's doing something. Otherwise, it's not.
Whether you Negroes recognize it or not, there is a revolution
going on. There are people using guns to defend their communities. Your lunches are not only going to be disrupted, your
whole lives are going to be disrupted, from today on."

Earlier in his talk, Murray had said that San Francisco State College was nothing more than a "nigger-producing factory," and that any black student who went along with the college program was "all effed up." He had then been interrupted by blacks in the crowd who urged him not to shrink from public profanity. Murray had capitulated. "The brothers said they are all 'fucked up,' " he explained.

Concluding, Murray said that as a consequence of the complaints he had cited, the BSU was going to stage a strike on November 6. October 28 had originally been set as the strike date, but when the BSU had failed to organize the entire black college community in time, the date had to be changed. It was important for the Black Student Union at State to have a successful strike, if for no other reason than that they wanted to live up to their public image: they considered themselves the vanguard organization in the United States, and they took special pride in their public record, which was almost devoid of idle threats.

The exclusively black organization had not emerged until the early sixties, when the number of black students at the college had decreased. Black students founded the Negro Student Association at that time, mainly in order to link the blacks on campus through social activities. Many of the organization's members were militant, but they rarely voiced their feelings, perhaps because the liberal college community would not have approved a black militant stance. Yet by the spring of 1966 the group had turned to African Nationalism.

That semester, short, skinny Jimmy Garrett came to San Francisco State from East Los Angeles City College in the black ghetto of Watts. Garrett said he had worked with Stokely Carmichael in Alabama and organized student groups in Los Angeles. He interrupted an NSA meeting at State in March of 1966 to declare, in reference to recently elected President Marianna Waddy, "First thing I want to know is why a woman is up there." Miss Waddy, who was far ahead of her time in wearing African garb, would never forgive Garrett. The strongly built, tall young woman soon stepped down from office to make room for Garrett, saying bitterly that small men always try to prove their superiority. Garrett objected to the name of the organization because it included the detested word "Negro," and Tricia Navara came up with the new title Black Student Union, which would soon be duplicated all over the country. Garrett, who wrote poetry, used the members' preoccupation with culture to bring them together for other ends. He soon moved into politics and made the BSU the most powerful pressure group on campus, successfully manipulating white student factions against one another. The organization also became a center for blacks who felt "just good" about banding together in an increasingly "hostile" environment. Garrett taught practical politics to future BSU leaders Benny Stewart, Jerry Varnado, future Black Panther Minister of Education George Murray and to Jack Alexis, who was admitted to the college through the BSU president's efforts. But the president's teachings were soon turned against him when his disciples ousted him after deciding that he did not discriminate in his manipulations. In the late summer of 1968, they created the Central Committee. This attempt to spread leadership among several predominant figures was another reason why Stewart asked Murray to speak in the cafeteria after the BSU's march across campus on October 28.

In his talk in the cafeteria, Murray had unintentionally broken the news of the forthcoming strike, and in addition had given new ammunition to those Californians who thought the black militants had gone too far. That afternoon Robert Smith's telephone rang constantly, as reporters inquired about the strike and about Smith's reaction to Murray's call for the blacks to arm. Smith, who was surprised to hear a march had taken place on campus, had little to say. But the Mayor of San

Francisco told an enthusiastic crowd of reporters and TV cameramen that if no law existed against urging students to bring guns on campus there should be one.

Three days later, on Thursday, the chancellor of the State Colleges, Glenn Dumke, who was in Washington, D.C., sent a telegram to President Smith ordering him to suspend George Murray. Smith surprised his close associates by defying Dumke, his superior. But they learned later that he had made his decision only after talking with the city's chief of police, who asked him to postpone the suspension until Friday afternoon to avoid an immediate and violent reaction to the news of the Black Panther's being fired. The police chief's fears were unfounded. The black students would not have reacted that Thursday, anyway. They were saving all their energy for the following Wednesday, November 6, when they planned to strike.

3

The Biggest Thing Yet

WHILE GEORGE MURRAY WAS SPEAKING IN THE CAFETERIA on October 28, tall, rugged-looking John Levin stood silently near the entrance, listening carefully. Earlier in the semester, Levin had tried to stir up conflict over ROTC between student activists and the administration. But during the last month, after several abortive efforts he had given up hope. He had also decided that, despite political pressure from the right, President Robert Smith would not be "stupid enough to fire Murray and cause a hassle."

Levin had come back to college in the fall looking also to the black students to start trouble. But he had decided that they too were waiting for the spring semester, if they had not already compromised with the administration.

Most likely they made a deal, he thought.

Now Levin wondered what the blacks' aim was. Earlier during the march, he had questioned a black student who could tell him only, "Today's the anniversary of Huey's arrest." But this explanation didn't satisfy Levin. If that were the only reason, why did the blacks file through the Ad Building? He was sure the march and speeches could not be the main event, as some college observers thought, but only an indication of something bigger to come. This gathering had not been publicized, and besides it was much too subdued to be the expected clash.

"What's going on?" a member of the Students for a Democratic Society inquired.

"I don't know," Levin replied quickly, irritated at being distracted from Murray's talk.

As Murray continued, both students found out what the blacks were up to.

When the Panther had finished talking, the leftist student, getting ready to leave the cafeteria, asked, "Well, what do you think, John?"

"I don't know," said Levin again, making his way through the crowd. But he added, "This might be the biggest thing yet."

Levin spent the afternoon after Murray's speech discussing the announced strike with two close associates in the Progressive Labor Party, Hari Dillon, an Asian Indian, and Bridges Randall, an American black. Although the three agreed that they did not fully trust the black student leaders, Levin and his friends decided that Progressive Labor should at least unofficially support the strike. That afternoon, Levin, Dillon, and Randall also arranged that the issue of the strike should be brought up at the next meeting of Students for a Democratic Society, scheduled for two days later.

Like other white leftist students who belonged to groups which had a definite ideology, such as PL's, Levin was active in the more flexible and exclusively student organization, SDS. At San Francisco State, as in other SDS chapters all over the United States, PL had rivaled with socialist organizations over dominance of SDS and had won.

PL's control of SDS had been achieved by the hard work of Levin and other party members. They volunteered, while others waited to be assigned. Over the semesters, PL members had made themselves indispensable to the running of SDS. The price PL paid for its power was dedication and discipline.

The main purpose of the next SDS meeting was to make final preparations for demonstrations on November 5, Election Day. SDS believed that the elections were a farce because all of the candidates supported the war in Viet Nam and none of them offered a satisfactory solution to the racial problem in the United States. As a student organizer for PL, Levin took great pride in seeing the radical student organization move closer to the position of his own party, which also included nonstudents. It was his job to see that such a move was made when he took over his position in 1966 after coming to San Francisco State.

Levin joined PL that year while he was a senior at Columbia University. He would prefer to think that his shift to Marxist politics was an intellectual choice based on his sense of fair play rather than an emotional response to the injustices perpetrated by the United States government. He adds that the war in Viet Nam, the invasion of the Dominican Republic by the Marines, and the general social malaise in the United States contributed to his political choice. PL had been founded in 1965 by Milton Rosen, who, after being ousted from the Communist Party, had organized what became known as the Progressive Labor Movement. Rosen accused the Communist Party bosses of revisionism, the same accusation the Chinese Communists had made against Kremlin leaders. PL's national leaders at first wanted their organization to be primarily a workers' party. But recruiting tables of this splinter group appeared on various campuses in the United States, and its strength ultimately came to lie with such student groups. Levin was aware of the party's existence at Columbia, but he did not become interested in it until the fall of '65. One day that semester, he saw a small clique of students encouraging protestors on Low Library steps to resist the police summoned by the administration. Levin learned afterward that these organizers belonged to PL, which was modeled after the Communist Party. At that time, the police did not carry billy clubs. "This sort of thing was new. They weren't prepared, so when students resisted, the cops retreated," Levin says. He believes that these were the precursors of confrontation politics.

Now, at San Francisco State three years later, as SDS decided to support the black students' strike, there was no opposition and very little discussion of the issue, just as Levin had expected. Because it was taken for granted at the college that anything the BSU planned would have the automatic support of SDS, the decision did not attract attention. The *Daily Gater* printed only one paragraph on it. But that insignificant story created a disagreement among black and white radicals which settled the question of who was in control of the strike.

The afternoon the story appeared, representatives of SDS, along with other leftist students, generally known as program students because of their involvement with extra-curricular community activities, were summoned to the BSU's dingy office. There, black student Jack Alexis, who acted as a liaison between the BSU and the college's whites, informed the white students that the BSU didn't like SDS's independent decision to support the strike, and asked that his organization be consulted in the future before public statements concerning it were made. While he had the upper hand, he also explained what his organization really expected from its white supporters.

Because of his rank and prestige within the college's activist circles, Levin had not gone to the BSU office that afternoon on such a summary order, but had sent three PL members who duly reported to him. When he heard that the BSU had rejected white support because, among other reasons, it would "confuse the issue," Levin retorted, "I don't give a flying fuck whether they want our support or not."

What really upset him was the blacks' demand for a formal coalition. They wanted white leftist organizations to be represented by a committee under the authority of the BSU Central

Committee. But Levin realized that it was too soon to assess the BSU's position, so he explained tentatively that the blacks' concern was the racial makeup of the strike. His temper cooling, he decided that this was a trivial matter which should be overlooked.

That weekend, fifteen SDS members belonging to the Worker-Student Alliance, which is a front for PL within SDS, met at their busiest "commune," 125 Steiner Street, where Levin instructed his loyal followers that under no circumstances should they form a coalition with program students and Trotskyists. He intended to stick firmly to this position at a meeting with non-SDS white leftist students scheduled for the following Monday, Levin explained. He added that he had been wrong earlier in predicting that President Robert Smith would not make the mistake of suspending Murray. Now Levin said that Smith's suspension of Murray the previous Friday, under direct orders from the chancellor, would attract additional student support for the strike. Levin did not mention it, but he was glad of an opportunity to show Murray he could keep a promise. The previous month the two had met on a plane bound to San Francisco from Los Angeles, where Levin had gone for a regional party meeting. Levin and Murray were both tired that night, but they briefly discussed Murray's status on campus. During their talk, Levin pledged full SDS support if the trustees should fire Murray under pressure from conservative Californians. The newspapers were already reporting on his activities and his public pronouncements. A local daily had publicized his trip to Cuba where Murray was reported to have said that every time a Viet Cong killed an American soldier it meant one less enemy for the black people of the United States.

On Monday morning, almost a month after his trip to Los Angeles, having parked his battered red Volkswagen on Junipero Serra as usual, four blocks from campus, Levin took out the new leaflets he had co-authored at 125 Steiner the previous day. It was still chilly, and he appreciated the heavy old coat he had brought from New York City. He walked down toward campus slowly and clumsily in his normal gait, as if he were flat-footed. It is hard to visualize him running. His walk seems a caricature of his personality, for he takes his time about everything, and talks the same way, slowly but confidently. Even during public speeches, he never changes his pitch and always chooses his words carefully. Levin's attempts to avoid sounding like a demagogue reflect his middle-class, liberal background rather than his current political convictions. Although he would never indulge in praising his parents, he mentions proudly that his father is never the pompous lawyer so many attorneys are.

Crossing Nineteenth Avenue, Levin saw rushing to their eight o'clock classes the students whom he wished to enlighten. He did not see any familiar faces in the cafeteria, half-full already, so he sat alone at a table near the entrance. As he drank his coffee and smoked a cigarette, he read over a leaflet which he had extracted from one of the three large manila envelopes he carried containing the day's message. Then he glanced through the *Daily Gater*, but instead of reading it soon stepped outside to buy the San Francisco *Chronicle* which he reads dutifully. By now it was close to nine o'clock and he could hit the students who would come to the cafeteria before their nine o'clock classes. Levin did not enjoy distributing leaflets, but he felt it was a good way to reach people.

The day's flyer began:

Why are the Trustees frantically trying to save us from George Murray? The Trustees, contrary to liberal myths, are not rabid right-wing fanatics, but competent, successful businessmen—like Dudley Swin, member of the Board of Directors of Del Monte. They are successful because they are able to extract super profits from the labor of Black, Brown and white workers.

It continued:

Corporation wizards who sit on the Board of Trustees are not there for their health, but to insure that the State Colleges meet their quotas of technicians and apologists to be the cogs in a system designed to serve the narrow interests of the corporate wealth. When George Murray says that students should not serve the oppressors, but *fight* them, he is a real threat to the role of higher education—that is, the role defined by the corporate interests of the Board of Trustees.

Standing in front of the cafeteria handing out leaflets offered some pleasant moments, when students stopped to talk or ask questions. Levin wished more people would do this. But others refused even to take the proffered information, and some accepted his leaflet only to register their opposition by tearing it up on the spot. Levin knew that some students took the sheet only out of courtesy, without having any intention of reading it, and that they would, as soon as they were out of sight, dispose of his attempts to educate them, in the nearest waste can.

But such incidents did not bother Levin any more. He had been exposed to this kind of reaction for the past three years. As far back as the fall of 1966, he had seen himself as an "agitator on the left wing of the Worker-Student Union," an organization of student employees at San Francisco State.

Levin's total record is impressive. Every semester since he came to San Francisco State, the college has been faced with a crisis. After founding a chapter of Progressive Labor in the fall of 1966, he joined the newly organized, moderate Organization of Student Employees, as a busboy in the student cafeteria. Immediately he began to urge increased benefits and security for student employees. But union officials were reluctant even to make such requests, having founded the union the previous semester only with great difficulty. With the help of the politically flexible SDS, which he had helped organize at San Francisco State the same semester, Levin and a handful of new PL Party members soon organized the Commons Boycott to protest the high price of meals and the low wages paid to student employees in the cafeteria. Levin and his PL comrades preferred to involve SDS rather than PL in student affairs. Being more flexible, SDS was popular with potential leftist students who distrusted old leftist organizations and those with strict ideologies just as much as they did Establishment political groups. PL preferred anonymity for tactical reasons too. It was not sure of how students would receive its policies, and at the time it was interested in agitating rather than recruiting. The party's efforts were successful. In the words of Donald Castleberry, a professor of political science who has taught at San Francisco State for twenty years, the Commons Boycott marked "the end of an era." Referring to "the sight of these students shouting at each other and at professors," Castleberry said, "I never knew the day would come when I would look forward to my retiring. . . ."

During the following semester, spring '67, the college witnessed its first sit-ins, peaceful and friendly demonstrations aimed at ending class ranking, the computing of grade-point averages in a descending list used by draft boards to determine which students to call. Both the boycott and the sit-ins were marked by student distrust of the administration's promises that a solution to their grievances would be worked out at a later date. PL members had soon overcome those who wanted to trust the administrators. During the same semester, the growing membership of SDS managed to prevent representatives of Dow Chemical from recruiting at San Francisco State. The central issue, the war in Viet Nam, had produced many new dissidents. Without openly arguing about it, PL veterans differed with these new SDS members on the causes of their mutual dissent: the former opposed the war purely for ideological reasons, while the latter argued from a moral standpoint. Newer members might object to class ranking because it discriminated against the poor who had to work and therefore had less time to study. They were fighting for a more equitable draft system. But Levin and his party felt that the draft should be abolished because it furthered the imperialistic purposes of the United States.

By the fall semester of 1967, the militant movement was well established at San Francisco State. Old civil rightists had already given up attempting to lead student movements, and, if they had not graduated, had retreated into the college's programs. The semester began with student politicians cynically predicting that the campus would soon blow up. The incidents which occurred provided new issues for John Levin and his supporters.

On November 6, fifteen black student militants went to the campus newspaper offices to register dissatisfaction with the paper's policy toward their race.

Black students had complained that the election of homecoming queen had been rigged against the BSU candidate, and editor Jim Vazcko had been partial to her white opponent in the newspaper. The black students had other grounds for complaint. On February 6, the previous semester, when Vazcko was sports editor, he had written a takeoff on student politicians including well-known blacks. Vazcko had depicted tiny Jimmy Garrett, then BSU Chairman, being carried on the ample shoulders of the BSU's representative on the Student Legislature, Marianna Waddy. Vazcko said, in part, "Mr. Garrett is head of the Black Student Union, better known as the BSU, and as usual one comes away with the feeling that he is trying to BS you." Terming Miss Waddy a "self-proclaimed upholder of all that is fair, decent and lilywhite (in politics)," the sports editor described her shouting "in unison with her shoulder pack: 'Us right or wrong; us good or bad; but us, us.'" Also, in the March 28 edition of the *Daily Gater*, in the same column, "Under the Bench," Vazcko had ridiculed Muhammad Ali, formerly Cassius Clay.

According to Vazcko's account, one of the blacks who entered his office said, "I want to talk to you, man."

Vazcko replied, "I'm on the phone, I'll be with you in a second."

"One of the Negroes ripped the phone from my hands and began beating me," Vazcko reported.

Black students stationed outside the editor's office, thinking that they were being attacked, immediately began to throw anything within reach. In a few seconds everyone in the room was swinging. When the blacks couldn't find anyone to hit, they threw papers, chairs and typewriters to the floor, overturned a few tables, and disappeared.

The visit to the *Daily Gater* office had been planned the previous Sunday afternoon at Garrett's home, where some of the BSU leaders had met casually. Among other topics, they had discussed hostile segments of the college community. Some of them mentioned instances of "racist professors" refusing to initiate courses dealing with black people. Others categorized entire departments as racist. Garrett, remembering Vazcko's attacks in print, subtly introduced his name. Over marijuana, they decided to visit "the racists" in a group to have a talk-confrontation and, by their mere physical presence, to shock "the enemy." They did not anticipate any physical attacks, nor making the local headlines.

All the mass media picked up the story, which stirred public outrage, especially when the time for disciplinary action passed and it was learned that the administration had taken no action against the black students. Then-President John Summerskill responded by immediately announcing that four students had been suspended, explaining that he had taken no further action because it would prejudice their case in court.

An unexpected event diverted public attention from the blacks. The campus "underground" newspaper *Open Process*, which catered to radicals and program students, published an "essay on sado-masochism" under a picture of its young, bearded author, who was clad only in a bunch of grapes in place of a fig leaf. The piece was dedicated to the Director of the Division of Health, Physical Education, and Recreation, "one of the leading intellectuals of our faculty." It began: "DOWN THE SELF HOLE. Alone I lift my supplicating cat in heat asshole . . ."

Eager to show that he was not the weak, permissive, liberal administrator he was often called, Summerskill quickly suspended the weekly, its editor, and the student who wrote the poem. The boyishly handsome, rosy-cheeked president soon received a phone call from the ACLU lawyer, who reminded him that his act was unconstitutional, and said that the courts would reverse his decision. When the college's lawyer concurred, Summerskill had no choice but to reinstate the suspended students.

Jimmy Garrett made an issue of this reinstatement, saying that San Francisco State was racist, and that Summerskill wouldn't have done the same for blacks. Garrett consistently repeated the same argument which, along with the suspension of *Open Process*, became the cause the white radicals were looking for.

John Levin and his associates continually held rallies in support of suspended students, both white and black. On December 6, 1967, SDS-PL, and others, under the acronym MAPS, Movement Against Political Suspension, demonstrated in front of the Administration Building to distract attention from a group of fifty young black students and ghetto youths who rampaged across campus. In bands of six to ten, they set small fires, beat up white students, and invaded the Bookstore, where they "liberated" merchandise under the fearful eyes of clerks. These incidents attracted national attention and boosted the morale of the white radicals whose earlier demonstrations, although similar to those held at the prestigious institutions of Stanford and the University of California at Berkeley, had not received similar notice. Now everyone on campus recognized that the blacks had become a force which could not be ignored, and the white radicals, being their allies, were thought to be partly responsible for the blacks' organization.

The spring semester of 1968 would not have been the same without Levin and his comrades. They kept political issues alive at San Francisco State by demonstrating, holding rallies, and distributing literature. With the war in Viet Nam escalating and conditions in urban centers worsening, there was much for SDS to criticize. The culmination of their efforts was the sit-ins of May, 1968, which resulted in the firing of President John Summerskill, who in distress accepted a job in Ethiopia. That spring, an increasing number of students joined the ranks of the militants after the police were called in. At the end of the semester, an estimated eight hundred students "sat in" to protest the presence of ROTC on campus, the firing of a Mexican-American professor, and the college's failure to admit larger numbers of unqualified nonwhite students. While these sit-ins were still at a peak, the semester came to an end, the students having obtained certain concessions, which were later to be rescinded. Levin officially ended the sit-ins by declaring a victory. "We will return next semester," he promised.

Now, the following semester, around ten o'clock on Monday morning, November 4, Levin was walking toward the library where a meeting of white student leaders with a BSU representative was scheduled. As he approached the beige building, which gives the impression of having been assembled in less than twenty-four hours, he thought about how he would argue against the BSU's Jack Alexis, and also against the white program students who followed any directive the blacks issued.

Program students were so-called because they worked for student programs designed to "bring about meaningful social change," as administrators explained to the public. One of the most well-known nationally was the Experimental College, instituted and funded by the Associated Students of San Francisco State. Student apologists pompously explained that the Experimental College was instituted because the other college was not responsive to the needs of students and was not relevant to their experience or lives. The students saw their creation, in the words of the President of the Associated Students, as a "quiet revolution from within." Here, they taught each other any subject they pleased. All that was needed was someone who assumed the role of teacher, and the pledge of a dozen or so students to sit through his classes. Among the unusual subjects taught at the Experimental College, the one which amused the public most was described in the September, 1967, issue of *Esquire* in an article by Herbert Wilner entitled "Zen Basketball at San Francisco State." Other courses which the public did not find amusing had become one of the excuses for a right-wing attack on State. The seminar on Guerrilla Warfare became the subject of a minor controversy in the Bay Area, to the dismay of those students who simply "wanted to conduct a bloodless revolution in peace."

Instituted in the same spirit were the Community Involvement and the Tutorial Programs. The program students saw themselves as reformists rather than revolutionaries. They made almost the same criticism of their society as the students affiliated with political groups, but they did not want to replace the whole system. Reformists and revolutionaries on campus tolerated each other's differences except in times of crisis. But Levin contemptuously calls the students affiliated with these programs the "junior administrators," because they receive a small salary for their work and cooperate with the administration of the college. Program students were often in close contact with black students who worked for the Tutorial Program or the Black Student Union. In dealing with black people, these white students took on an understanding role, always forgiving what they would not tolerate in whites, and readily reacting with guilt to any implication that blacks were not being treated equally in this society. The blacks exploited the program students' weaknesses by letting this guilt fester, especially if it did not interfere with their own interests.

Levin resented such relationships, and he was determined to take a stand which he felt would give him and his organization some say in leading the strike. His tactic was to stall any action until that afternoon, when a mass meeting was scheduled. When he arrived at Room G-1, the site of many heated student and faculty meetings, program students were already discussing the strike informally with BSU's emissary, Jack Alexis. Unlike other BSU leaders, Alexis adapted himself rather easily to his dual role as go-between and militant black. In the position of go-between, he was cordial and friendly to whites, but in the latter role he spoke to them as infrequently and as briefly as possible.

Alexis came to the United States from Trinidad in 1963. Like many other foreign students, he had intended to study engineering and return to his native land. Both he and his parents expected that he would go to work for Shell Oil Company where his father is employed as a sales manager, that he would continue in the middle-class tradition, moving up in the social scale, just as his father had done in his younger days. But Alexis discovered that he did not have to become an engineer to earn a living and be accepted as a respectable member of society, and less than one year after his arrival in the United States he decided to major in the humanities. After graduating from the College of San Mateo, a two-year institution, he transferred to San Francisco State. Through his new friends in the Bay Area, he had met Garrett, who had arranged his admission. Alexis had already terminated his romance with a Danish girl he had met in San Mateo—he was later to marry a BSU girl at San Francisco State—and his conversion to a black militant soon became complete.

Through genuine concern for his race and his friendship with strong man Jimmy Garrett, Alexis rose in the hierarchy of the Black Student Union. Unlike other black militants, he at no time completely severed ties with white students, nor did he become an extremist in outlook or appearance. It was only under pressure from BSU members during the organization's most militant period that he disassociated himself from white students in public. Alexis wears conservative clothes, and speaks gently. Although his language is often idiomatic and he uses American expletives, he still talks like a West Indian. He is six feet two, one hundred and ninety pounds, and his manners remind one of a young African statesman. His tone and facial expression suggest that he is more interested in convincing than in imposing his views on those with whom he is talking.

Alexis is always worried about wasting time, but he will gladly spend hours discussing Negro history or current issues, if he feels that he is participating in a serious exchange of ideas. He would rather be working for the BSU, tutoring black students, or educating himself by reading. Once, having felt that he had wasted several days in a row, Alexis said he wished he were locked up in jail where he could be reading and writing.

Because it was mainly Alexis' idea to involve the white students in the forthcoming strike, he was the most appropriate member of the BSU to attend the Monday morning meeting. In his customarily persuasive tone, Alexis began to talk a little louder to the students gathered in Library G-1. Now the gathering began to take on a formal aspect. He was reiterating his position, which he had painfully explained to the white group summoned to BSU headquarters three days earlier. But now it was understood that the whites would be active in the strike without participating in its leadership.

"You've got to organize," he said in his Trinidad accent, "and form a coalition. You waste lots of time discussing things, and you do little. Have a committee elected that will decide for the group." Alexis had the BSU model in mind. He wanted the whites to centralize power in a body similar to the BSU Central Committee—one which would hand down decisions with a minimum number of mass meetings.

Levin raised objections to undemocratic style, self-righteously saying, "We can't do that. Students have to decide what they want to do, and our strength lies there." But this logic led nowhere. The group eventually agreed that the subject should be brought up again at the mass meeting to be held that afternoon.

The next question was the central theme for rallying white student support for the strike. Levin made a suggestion immediately. "I think," he began, "we can get the students to support the strike around the issue of racism."

"That's too amorphous," Peter Shapiro replied nervously. He was the managing editor of *Open Process*, which was also considered part of the programs. "We should try to make an issue out of the powerlessness of the students," he said, referring to efforts by the chancellor of the state colleges to establish tighter control over student governments throughout the state college system.

This one-hour meeting resulted in only one decision, that the time of the afternoon meeting should be kept at the scheduled hour of two o'clock instead of one, as had been suggested.

Levin left the library confident that the afternoon meeting would bring about the defeat of the program students. He was strongly against putting all the white radical students of San Francisco State under the authority of the blacks, whose aims were too blatantly capitalistic for him. Approaching the cafeteria, he noticed his associates standing at the PL table near the entrance. Over a cup of coffee, the three discussed the strategy for that afternoon.

Levin recounted what had taken place at the morning meeting. He said proudly that, as he had promised, no decision had been made. Since it was getting close to noon, the trio left the cafeteria and headed toward the Speakers' Platform where a rally was scheduled to take place.

As one of the speakers at the rally, Levin bent over the podium, leaning on his elbow, cigarette in hand. In his usual monotone, he defended violence, saying it was "an abstract term."

He asked what the liberals would have suggested George Baskett, a black, do before he was killed by an off-duty San Francisco policeman a few weeks earlier.

"Should he have tried to sit down and say to the cop, 'Let us reason together?'" Levin asked.

As other speakers before him, he heartily condemned the administration for George Murray's suspension.

Around one o'clock, the number of listening students had dwindled, and soon only the organizers of the rally were left. Other students who had been sitting on the grass and enjoying their lunches gradually disappeared too, and the central area of San Francisco State began to look the way it does in mid-afternoon. By three o'clock it would be desolate and quiet, a group of inexpensive constructions where occasionally students could be seen walking from one building to another. Levin walked back to the cafeteria with his comrades. That day he had not attended his classes, but didn't feel he had missed anything. The only reason he was registered in school, anyway, was to organize students. He found school boring. Even when he attended classes, it was to generate discussion, raise issues pertinent to social change, and acquaint students with the Marxist-Leninist thinking of the Progressive Labor Party. After finishing his fourth cup of coffee that day and opening his second pack of cigarettes, he went to the Gallery Lounge, accompanied by his associates.

As he walked in, shortly before two o'clock, he saw some one hundred students scattered about, talking, reading newspapers, studying, or taking afternoon naps. Not all these students had come to attend the meeting. The Lounge, the only place of its kind on campus for student use, was their pride and also their shame. Every few months, the committee in charge of the student lounge decorated it with student paintings, sculpture, or photographs, and occasionally exhibited the work of non-students through the courtesy of a local benefactor or art gallery. The Lounge has a temporary air about it which makes it resemble the offices or storage room of a used-car lot, built in the shortest possible time to hasten the period of profit-making. A box in shape, it has two doors in the middle of either end and no windows.

As other students arrived, those who had been in the Lounge to relax began to leave. Some stayed behind, curious to see what the meeting would be about, but left shortly afterward, having either staisfied their curiosity or become bored. Those with an interest in campus politics remained. Everyone knew what the arguments behind the conflicting viewpoints would be, and that two factions—the reformists and the revolutionaries—would emerge.

The PL faction of SDS, as every other organization, wanted to control all the white students supporting the strike, and disagreements on tactics and ideological differences resulted in a three-and-a-half-hour meeting, which might have lasted even longer had it not been that a few blacks attended the meeting to make sure it didn't drag on. The program students dominated the meeting at the beginning, mainly by occupying the chair. But, about halfway through, the better organized Progressive Labor Party won out by replacing the chairman with one of its own members. At the beginning, PL members had not been able to pack the meeting, but they soon summoned friends and sympathizers from classes all over campus and called for a reelection of the chairman. The program students then realized that the BSU's blessings and the presence of its emissaries were not enough to control the now close to 250 white students. Levin and his friends had posted their sympathizers among every twenty or thirty students to create a unified voice. He was assisted in the effort to crush the program students by non-PL members of SDS and by Trotskyists, who at this point agreed with him that it was by confrontation politics that the strikers could gain maximum student support.

"We've got to get out of the bag of confrontation because the administration and the trustees have superior military and tactical power," Jim Willems of the Experimental College said, expressing the feelings of other students from the programs. "We have to talk in terms of reforming the system. We have to strike this university because there is no more space to work here. The trustees have decided to shut the students down. We have to set up our own college, our own classes and reform things," Willems continued patiently, sincerely believing that he might change opinions among those who were gathered in the Gallery Lounge. The black students claimed that they did not want to force the administration to call in the police and the program students agreed with them. But the blacks knew their own unrevealed plans were sure to bring the police on campus.

PL had not talked openly of using confrontation tactics, but this was clearly understood in constant references to direct action and mobilization of masses. PL was not interested in the issue of Black Studies or in Nathan Hare. Nor was PL interested in an autonomous Black Studies Department. The Marxist-Leninist organization wanted to use the strike to convert students to its doctrine, by first getting them to admit that the system, which includes every institution in this country, serves the interest of only a handful of Americans. Then PL would offer its version of the Marxist-Leninist alternative.

As the meeting dragged on, Jack Alexis warned SDS in a threatening tone that it had better shorten its theoretical discussions about the masses and just do as it was told by the blacks. "If SDS sticks with its same tactics we may have to leave SDS out," he explained. His threat hit a very sensitive nerve. PL could not afford to let the disagreement between SDS and the BSU become a public issue in 1968. This would have shattered SDS's progressive image and decreased its attractiveness to potentially leftist students. More important, there was always the fear of being classified as racist, which Levin had to consider, for he knew that too many white students in the Gallery Lounge on that Monday felt that racist was the worst attribute they could be given.

"We've seen at Columbia, Berkeley, and here that SDS mobilizes people and leaves them hanging there," Alexis went on. "We are past that point. We are working to build a continuing movement, and in this respect all we want from you is to organize the student workers in the Library, the Bookstore, and the Commons."

Alexis made these criticisms in an effort to stop the discussion of abstract theories for which neither he nor the program students had any taste. As soon as he had finished explaining what the black students wanted from the whites, a student devoted to the Progressive Laborites in SDS, one considered highly reliable by Levin and his friends, who was sitting on the floor some fifteen feet away from Levin, stood up and began reciting the PL line: "We have power, and when we mass together we can win demands. We must fight for a campus that serves the needs of this community and the people. We should be here to rectify the raw deals being handed to the special admittees, to people like Juan Martinez and Nathan Hare."

This student was working hard to be admitted to the PL Party, which requires applicants to prove themselves by faithful labor and consistent attendance at study sessions.

A spokesman for the programs, Peter Shapiro, retorted thoughtfully and with marked calm, "It's true that we have power while we're in the Administration Building, but the moment we leave we get screwed."

At this point Levin took the floor and explained how direct action tactics yield results: "As a matter of fact," he said, "last

May, from a handful of students we managed to mobilize over 800 who are willing to come back and struggle with us." And from then on, it was arithmetic. If a few mobilized 800, 800 could mobilize more, with the assistance of the police and the administration, who would anger others by taking extraordinary measures in time of crisis.

Alexis rose again and, as if talking to military subordinates, said that the whites should organize a communications committee which would act as a liaison group between black leaders and white students. Somewhat resentful and not afraid to show it, an SDS member began to argue with him.

"We don't have any duty to take orders from the BSU," he said, to which a BSU member sitting at the other end of the room responded, his hands in his pockets, "Then why are you striking on the sixth? Why don't you strike on the seventh then?"

After deliberation, the students finally voted to support the ten BSU demands and to join the strike. They elected a communications committee, and they vowed that "under no circumstances" would they force the administration to call police on campus.

4

What Do You Suggest, Dr. Smith?

THE BSU'S STRIKE CALL WAS TO BLACK EMPLOYEES OF THE college as well as to students. As Jerry Varnado said later, "It was very important for us that all the blacks at the college walk out on November 6." Having all the blacks at San Francisco State strike would show the college community, particularly the administration, that the young blacks spoke for more than their own generation.

There were other reasons for the strike besides display. Despite the power they had secured, black student leaders were haunted by doubts about the BSU's strength. Internal dissension precipitated by white students' demonstrations and sit-ins during the previous semester had led to disagreements in the black organization and the threat that splinter groups would emerge. A few BSU members wanted to support the sit-ins and involve the Union, at least behind the scenes. Another faction, led by Jerry Varnado, "didn't want to have anything to do with whites." The BSU was never even informally involved in the dispute between white students and the administration, but the sit-ins were the immediate cause of Jimmy Garrett's loss of the BSU chairmanship and the confusion to which it led. Garrett had made enough enemies within the organization to be voted out easily after being formally accused of "wheeling and dealing with the enemy" and of mishandling BSU funds.

Garrett's roommate had reported that the diminutive BSU chairman was "too friendly" with John Summerskill, then-president of the college. Summerskill would phone, asking for "Jimmy." When Garrett wasn't at home, his roommate would ask who was calling, and Summerskill would reply, "Tell him John called." Remembering this offense of Garrett's, one black student says, "Imagine! There was nothing whatever to talk about. He was the enemy. What was there to say? It would be just like me getting friendly with Thomas Cahill," the San Francisco chief of police. As further evidence of Garrett's friendship with the college president, the black students cited incidents of the December 6, 1967, disturbances when Garrett played an important role in restraining the militant blacks who otherwise "could have burned the place down."

Those who opposed Garrett, including George Murray, Varnado, and Benny Stewart, had decided that over the past two years Garrett had successfully manipulated everyone in the organization for his own selfish ends. Furthermore, he had been making promises in the name of the BSU which had never been kept. Garrett had convinced a visiting professor, author John Gerassi, that some whites should be arrested to "take the heat off" those blacks who had been charged with assault on the editor of the student daily. In return, the arrested whites were to get the BSU's support, a promise which Garrett chose to forget, even when an enthusiastic Gerassi got himself arrested. It wasn't so much the unkept promise that upset the BSU leaders—they didn't care whether a promise to white Gerassi was kept or not—but Garrett's "nerve" in speaking in the name of the organization without consulting a single member.

Although Garrett was ousted from the BSU at the end of the spring semester, 1968, and almost literally driven out of San Francisco, hard feelings had remained. West Indian Jack

Alexis, also suspect because of his association with whites, was identified as a Garrett supporter. That summer, Alexis thought seriously about organizing a splinter group, hoping to derive its membership from non-American blacks and to form a coalition with white sympathizers.

To many college observers, it seemed that the blacks had settled down after the violent attack on the *Gater* editor and the terrorizing on campus during the fall semester, 1967. To the white radicals, it seemed that the blacks had "copped out." To the self-conscious and relatively new black student organization, these observations by outsiders meant that it had become weak and that a reassessment of its strength was necessary, particularly when membership was dropping. But the immediate cause of the strike was the proposed Black Studies Department.

During the previous summer, Varnado and other influential BSU members had carried on lengthy talks with administrators on the subject of a proposed Black Studies Department. Under two different presidents, the administration had already made some progress toward establishing such a department. Earlier that year, then-president John Summerskill, despite objections from faculty members, including one black, had hired Nathan Hare, recently fired from Howard University, a Negro institution, for his militancy. A former boxer, Hare had taught at Howard for two years, where he was popular with the new militant black students, among them Stokely Carmichael. The son of an Oklahoma cotton farmer, Hare was one of fourteen children. He had come to Howard from the University of Chicago, after obtaining his Ph.D. in sociology. Hare had spent the spring of 1968 at San Francisco State writing a program for the proposed Black Studies Department, and—despite faculty misgivings that the program was not sufficiently academic—it had been accepted. The standard procedure for establishing a new department at San Francisco State includes six steps, the last of which is review by the board of trustees. In previous dealings with the administration, the Black Student Union had always managed to have ordinary procedures bypassed. Now black students expected similar treatment in a more important area. Moreover, some black student leaders believed that they had already gone through "normal channels" only to be rejected. These students argued that their first attempt had been made in March, 1967, when they presented the Instructional Policies Committee and later the Academic Senate with a proposal for a Black Studies Institute.

With previous failures in mind, various members of the BSU Central Committee met with administrators during the summer of 1968, demanding a department. Then-President Robert Smith candidly, but not very tactfully, told them he did not think the proposed department was appropriate. His objection was similar to that of John Bunzel, a political science professor who, in an article to appear that fall in the quarterly *Public Interest*, argued that the Black Studies Department proposed by Nathan Hare and the BSU was more political than academic.

When talks between the BSU leaders and the administration proved unsuccessful, Jerry Varnado suggested to the Central Committee one day in August that they involve the well-known and established members of San Francisco's black community in the controversy. The task of inviting the black community leaders to meet with the administration of the college was assigned to Elmer Cooper, a recently hired black administrator who had been made associate dean of students. Many felt that the twenty-eight-year-old Cooper had been hired to pacify the blacks and to act as a liaison between them and the administration.

One of the San Franciscans Cooper told about the black students' problems was Assemblyman Willie Brown. Brown, a graduate of San Francisco State, represents the racially integrated Eighteenth District, which includes the Haight-Ashbury. He promptly arranged a meeting between black community leaders and Robert Smith and his staff. The group was unable to come to any agreement. A second meeting was set for the afternoon of Friday, September 13.

On that occasion, a group of some twenty-five students, including BSU leaders, walked up the stairs of the Administration Building to attend the meeting. With giggles and loud laughs, they were talking about the roles they intended to play: some were to "act crazy and foolish" and threaten the administrators; some were to "be intelligent" and "restrain the brothers." These parts had been rehearsed at the BSU offices that day, and the administrators' anticipated reactions found very amusing. The previous night at a Central Committee meeting, it had been decided that the black students, as they had done before, would make an attempt to divide the various administrators.

The older members of the San Francisco black community were already in the conference room when the students arrived. That room, later to be converted into three offices to house the new president's assistants and their secretaries, is next to the president's office and connected to it by a door. Its bare, shiny, beige walls remind one of those in the college's classrooms. The tables in the room, at that time arranged in T-shape, were barely spacious enough to seat those who were already inside. Behind the tables, at opposite corners of the room, the flags of the United States and the State of California hung on poles. Exchanging smiles and laughing, the students entered, but at the sight of the administrators they became serious. Inside the room, chatting ceased as the students entered and began to spread out, posting themselves against the walls. Edward X, the campus Black Muslim recruiter, approached the white administrators. "You white devils should read *Muhammad Speaks*," he told them, holding out his papers. He sold a few copies of the Muslim weekly, while the black students looked on approvingly.

Jerry Varnado made his way through the congested room

and stood at the head of the T-shaped table. He took out of his hip pocket a sheet of paper containing a list of books on famous blacks, which he had picked up in the BSU office earlier. Pretending it contained a list of the administrators' names, he began to make introductions. Some of the black students were attending the meeting for educational purposes, to see the administration racists and learn how to handle them. The neophytes were also present to assist their black brothers in obtaining what they felt was their due: a Black Studies Department at San Francisco State.

"That over there is Dog Robert Smith. He is an enemy of the people. He is the president of the college. But only in name," Varnado said in his Southern drawl. Smith sat silent and expressionless. To approving mumbles among the students, Varnado continued, "That over there is Donald Garrity. He is a criminologist. Three times a week he teaches at the Police Academy. He is the one who has the power in this administration. He is an enemy of the people, too." Consulting his "list" again, Varnado introduced Dean Fedder as "the friend of the people." "Fedder liked that," Varnado remembered later. Pleased at seeing the dean fall for his ruse, which was intended to divide the administrators by imposing varying roles on them, Varnado went on. "That cat over there is Don Scoble. Because he is working for Dog Smith, he is also an enemy of the people." These extraordinary introductions took Scoble by surprise. An aspiring young administrator, recently promoted assistant to the president, Scoble had just begun to get acquainted with what his new job entailed.

When Varnado had finished, President Robert Smith, taking great pains, explained to the gathered community representatives what he thought the problem was. Smith had been with the institution for twenty years. He had been appointed president of San Francisco State in June of 1968, after being one of five appointees suggested for the post by the college's Presidential Selection Committee. That group was composed of five professors—among them S. I. Hayakawa—who represented different factions of the college faculty. The committee had chosen him from among fifty or so candidates in the one month after John Summerskill was fired. Upon the suggestion of the chancellor, the trustees had then appointed Smith, for his reputation as a tough educator and for his conservativism, attributes which are not obvious. Those who know him well immediately point out, in considering his career, that he is correct and fair and not as conservative as some people think. He is also a pleasant and gentle man. Short and stocky—he is five feet eight inches tall and weighs 190 pounds—he often colors his conversation with humorous remarks. He always speaks informally and wears colorful and inexpensive, but not unfashionable clothes. He was born in Illinois in 1916, the son of a farmer father and a teacher mother, the second of three children, all of whom became teachers. At Northern Illinois State University, Smith received his teaching credentials, the only major he could undertake without cost, and then came to Stanford, where he obtained a doctorate in education. In the middle of the spring semester of 1948, while writing his dissertation, Smith began his long career at San Francisco State.

Now his introduction to the gathered blacks and administrators was interrupted: "As of right now, why don't you have Black Studies . . . ?" Anticipating the rest of the question, Smith also broke in, to explain patiently, "Why don't we have a Black Studies program? Well, I think that part of it is the question of understanding the differences in interpretation of what is involved in Black Studies and, secondly, the problem of trying to manage all of the staff demands and, thirdly, the need to get the program developed, laid on the books and approved through our curriculum committee, which doesn't ordinarily function during the summer." Smith's tone was sympathetic, but somewhat tired. He always stops periodically in talking, as if he were short of breath. "And the program has to be approved for the college by the trustees," he went on. "As a result of the discussions of the last couple of weeks, the last time we met, Don Garrity recommended that we propose . . ." Smith stopped for a moment. He leaned forward to look at Donald Garrity, a few chairs away, the silver tips of his bolo tie hitting the table.

In an effort to clarify Smith's remarks, Garrity volunteered a shorter and simpler statement. He had been at San Francisco State for over ten years, most of that time as an administrator, and he knew all about procedure. To the black students, his taking over now seemed further evidence that he was indeed the one in charge. Garrity seemed to be explaining that Black Studies was presently composed of courses which were officially in other departments and that it was necessary to develop a separate series of courses which would constitute the program of the proposed department.

"Are you saying that the Black Studies Department cannot be established without a program? Or are you saying that . . ." Black student Nesbitt Crutchfield was asking his questions in determined tones. A former Air Force officer from Michigan, he was disenchanted with the system, like the other militant blacks.

Before he could finish, Nathan Hare interrupted. His words tumbled out: "The word *program* confuses the issue. Use the word *major* to refer to a major. We have a program that people from all over the country come here trying to get some advice on . . ."

"I think you have a program because you can enlist the aid of members of the community, because black people are here." Assemblyman Willie Brown had taken over in an attempt to bring the issues into focus. Becoming calm again, Nathan Hare settled back into his characteristic position, arms folded across his chest, leaning back in his chair. His face showed no emotion as he waited to see what Brown would say.

"You have a Black Studies program because you can enlist the aid of the black people, because you asked us to come,"

Brown continued. Mutters of "Right on!" greeted his remarks.

"To talk about putting in a Black Studies program . . . I would rather hear *yes* or *no!*" Brown said. Then he hesitated, as if to counteract his harshness. "This is one of the reasons why those of us in the community some time ago have gotten off . . ."

"But . . ." Garrity interrupted.

"I would like to speak," Willie Brown broke in again, raising his voice a little louder. "The country blows up, everybody is involved with racism—'What's going to happen? How do we save our society?' And yet we can't get a commitment to cut through bureaucratic nonsense and establish a Black Studies program. It would appear that in 1968 if the black students on this campus are asking for something, they would get it. Period! Because our society is blowing up because black people have not gotten anything. And to sit here and go through these ponderous procedures really begs the question and asks for a confrontation . . ."

As Brown was talking, Reverend A. Cecil Williams, one of the community delegates, interrupted, perhaps to cut off what might have been interpreted as threats. "Let's make some differentiation here," he said. "We're really talking about a Black Studies Department, right?"

Different voices replied in unison, "Right!"

He continued, "Black Studies Department, that's what you're talking about, right? Because you already have a program."

"I think it's important, though, for us to know what we're talking about," Garrity said enthusiastically.

"We know what we're talking about," Crutchfield said, enunciating every word clearly. "We have an ongoing, viable, strong, stable Black Studies program. We want a strong, viable Black Studies Department. The program—or the major—can come in 1969."

What was loosely being termed a *program* consisted of a series of courses dealing with various subjects from the black man's perspective. Almost two years earlier, the black students at San Francisco State had taken the opportunity offered by the Experimental College to introduce these courses. The free Experimental College was financed almost entirely by the student government. Black students, attempting to create courses "relevant" to their lives, had used little critical judgment, sometimes replacing white racist myths with equally ridiculous fantasies. As most of the BSU leaders were to recognize, many of the courses which emphasized blackness were primarily therapeutic.

After two semesters at the experimental stage, some of these courses were transferred to various departments of the State College with the help of sympathetic white professors. By the spring of 1967, there were enough of these courses offered to warrant the BSU's request that the College establish a Black Studies Institute. But the request that they drew up for the Instructional Policies Committee did not satisfy the professors who read it. Reminiscing about the general impression the black students' request created, one of them says, "It sounded a bit strange to us. Black this, black that, and our reaction was 'Black horseshit.' "

The black students were determined that they would not give up. By fall, 1967, the administration had begun to think of the BSU as a redoubtable force, to be managed rather than confronted, especially after the student editor of the campus newspaper was beaten up and, exactly one month later to the day, the campus terrorized by groups of black youths. Also, the BSU's control of white activists had noticeably increased. It seemed to many like a black conspiracy. In this atmosphere, then-BSU Chairman Jimmy Garrett had been able to make President John Summerskill hire Nathan Hare, who had been fired from the prestigious Negro institution, Howard University. Hare was under the impression that he had been brought to San Francisco State to work on a program which would be put into effect immediately, rather than to pacify impatient black students. His principal task that semester consisted of writing an eight-page conceptual proposal for a Black Studies Department. Coming to San Francisco State College eager to work, he had been told instead to take it easy. Hare was not quite sure of how to interpret his white colleagues' attitude. But, with time, it became clear to him that he was not welcomed wholeheartedly, and he was to say later, "I made a big mistake by coming out here."

Now that he was at the college, he had decided to put up a good fight. Hare, who once beat up his brother to prove to the neighborhood children that he could do so, says he has learned that "you can't be a patsy and let people walk over you." At this meeting, in the presence of the black students who had become his close friends, he expressed all his anger and frustration, talking so quickly that he could hardly be understood: "We cannot work with departments that don't want to work with us, departments that are opposed to the program. I think the issue—even maybe genuine to a certain extent—the issue of bureaucracy or the pressure of time is really a reluctance by the administration to face the conservative forces, the hostile forces within the college who don't want the Black Studies program. And yet it's pushed off to an issue like bureaucracy when actually it's just the fact that people don't want the program and the administration doesn't want to fight them."

"Well, that isn't what I sense," Smith replied sympathetically, sitting straight up in his chair. "For instance, the deans have committed themselves to a Black Studies Department when a program organized for black studies has been approved. Now, all right, let's say that maybe that's not the only way it could be done. But we don't propose that the deans go back on that commitment. I don't propose it. And Garrity is recommending that we get a Black Studies Department established."

Crutchfield intervened again: "I'd like to add one other thing. We've been throwing around words like *commitment.*

We're not asking for commitments any more. We've had long exposure to everyone telling us how committed they are. What we're talking about is the establishment—very simple—the establishment of a Black Studies Department. And that can be done by an executive order today, by President Doctor Robert Smith."

Crutchfield then told the administrators to compress the steps involved in establishing a department and to leave the blacks alone. According to this plan, Hare would head the department, working in close cooperation with the BSU. No disagreements were anticipated. In the past, Hare had told the students that he would do anything they wanted because the department was the result of their efforts.

"I'd like to say something." Varnado was speaking to the gathering in general where everyone was talking at once. He was at the head of the T-shaped table, but he hadn't participated in the discussion yet. "I'd like to say something," he repeated, "about what you've been talking about." When nobody paid any attention to him, he pointed his finger at Smith and Garrity and said loudly: "O.K. You better let me talk. Dig it?" Everyone was quiet.

"We already have a program, but we don't have a department," Varnado said. "What is happening is that we're going to departments trying to get classes that we have requested, and these are the obstacles we're running into now. The departments won't accept the courses the way we have them written." He was alluding to departments which would not allow the setting up of black studies courses, to be taught by black students. Each department allows its members to initiate a class on an experimental basis after preparing a course description and a reading list. "One of the departments giving us trouble is this man's department," Varnado went on, tapping his index finger on the table. "He is the Dean of the School of Behavioral and Social Sciences, you know." The administrator Varnado was pointing out was DeVere Pentony, whom Smith had appointed as his assistant just after becoming president, when he decided that the regular staff was not large enough to run the college efficiently during difficult times. As Dean Pentony was attempting to object, Varnado raised his hands and, turning his head to the left, shut his eyes and waved his hands, saying, "Hold it, hold it, hold it, hold it."

"Now there are some other dogs giving us trouble too. Brother Hare told us that it was you, and you over there, the whole School of Behavioral and Social Sciences Economics, Psychology, and all that stuff. You might be," Varnado paused for a second, holding his lapel. "You might be in the frame of mind where you want to give us two or three courses." Now he was pointing a finger at Fenton McKenna, Dean of the School of Creative Arts. "This other cat McKenna. We're running around to different departments [in the School of Creative Arts] trying to get courses that we need, when we could have the department and all this would be unnecessary. All of it would be unnecessary. This man here knows it," Varnado said, pointing to Smith. "He came out the other day and said to me that he didn't support the Black Studies program and he knows it, this one right here, Robert Smith."

"I said I had not made a commitment to the Black Studies program," Smith said firmly. "We said now that a commitment had been made. I said I had not made a commitment to a Black Studies Department because at that time we had not received a program that had been approved and because at that time that was the recommendation of the academic vice-president. Since that time, we have said that we will support and gain approval for a Black Studies Department. Then the issue becomes one of a program that needs to be approved." Smith shuffled the papers in front of him and shook the ashes from his unlit cigar. "I just have to say that, for the welfare of the people in the area of black studies and in the area of the additional ethnic studies programs, that no doubt will come along. It's important that we find a way of getting approval of a pattern of courses that are acceptable both to those of you who are concerned in black studies and it's important that we get the support of the college, because of the problem of trying to maintain a college in which a variety of racial and ethnic groups can work together in higher education."

"O.K., O.K., O.K.," Varnado said, as if he had heard enough. "Now let me say something."

"Do you recognize what I am trying to say?" Smith asked.

"I understand what you're trying to say," Varnado replied. "Now this man here," he went on, pointing at Pentony, "tries to subvert. His department, first of all, attempts to subvert the Black Studies program. One of the ways he does that is if courses come through for us in the Psychology Department or in the Social Science Department, what he does is you don't ever find him. He went off and found a Japanese Tom and a Negro Tom to coordinate the courses. Therefore our animosities, which he takes off himself, are directed toward them. He didn't consult anybody about hiring this fellow over in the Psych Department. He didn't consult anybody about hiring this fellow in the Social Science Department." Varnado was now expressing the anger of the BSU leaders who had expected to be teaching the new courses themselves.

Pentony, who seemed rather amused at these charges, said smilingly that the allegations weren't correct, and added, "Everybody has a different point of view, I suspect." He told the members of the black community that he had done everything he could for the Black Studies Department. "As a matter of fact," he said, "I could be accused by some of my colleagues of taking staff time from their departments and giving it to Black Studies, but I am used to that kind of thing." Pentony then promised that he would personally recommend the department to the chancellor and the trustees because "the preparation that Professor Hare has been doing and the general idea of a

Black Studies curriculum and a Black Studies Department makes a lot of sense in this era, and I think this college ought to move to get that accepted as quickly as it possibly can."

Crutchfield, who says that before joining the Air Force he believed that "this system offered equal opportunity for everyone and that all black people had to do was try harder," interrupted again, in accented syllables. "Dr. Smith, may I ask my question once more? And I would like to address myself to you because you are the president. All my colleagues keep telling me that all the power rests with Don Garrity, but I want to address my question to you," he told the smiling Smith. Crutchfield, who had assumed the role of an "intelligent and understanding" student, as opposed to Varnado, who was playing the "foolish and reckless" role, was referring to a question Smith had asked the group earlier, "Do you want us by executive order to install a program of Black Studies without any effort whatsoever to get the rest of the college community to accept it?" The black students had answered, "We do." Crutchfield now asked, "How soon can we get a Black Studies Department? No program. Programs will come. We all know that we are all committed to it. We all said that. How soon? Can you answer that question?"

Smith took on a businesslike air. Turning to Garrity, he asked, "Do you think the Senate Executive Committee needs to review this?"

A quick survey among the administrators did not yield a conclusive reply, and Smith asked the black delegation, "Do you want me to make a press release after this meeting and say that there will be a Black Studies Department here?"

"Only if there is one," Willie Brown answered quickly.

"All right, we have a department," Smith replied.

But he explained that the program still had to go through ordinary channels, "and get the approval of the trustees as quickly as we can get concurrence. I do not propose myself at this point to enunciate programs of any kind in the college that have completely bypassed the institutional structure, and I don't quite see why it is necessary."

Exasperated, Brown said in a shriek, "How many courses have been established where the majority of the people involved with that course were asking for it? No, let me finish," he said, shaking his head, as various administrators attempted to explain their position. "You know, every time someone throws out the word *racism*, very nice white people cringe. And the reason why we talk about a racist society and racist presidents and racist institutions at this point is that ten percent of the State," he said, referring to the black population of California, "is asking for a Black Studies program. Black students on this campus, to a person, are asking for Black Studies. Now I'm certain that geology courses have been set up, and all types of esoteric courses and departments that represent maybe one one-hundredth of the constituency of the state of California. Yet here we have black people unanimously asking you to put something in for black people, put it in now, put it in this afternoon, and you tell us about ponderous procedures. How can I conclude anything else but that this is a racist institution? If Dr. Hare is here for Black Studies he should be in a Black Studies Department. Period. Now! I can remember going to college where courses were set up that didn't have a damned thing to do with us. Somebody who didn't even know what a Negro was was teaching something on Negro history."

"Right on!" shouted the students leaning against the walls. Brown's words expressed their frustrations. The rejection of some of their proposed courses was taken to mean that the white professors wanted to teach the courses themselves.

Encouraged by the shouts, Brown began to speak a little louder, moving to the edge of his chair. "Here we have black people sitting, unanimously asking you. Look, people come out of the community because the students say, 'We want a Black Studies Department,' and yet we have to go through all this. You know what we say? 'The hell with it.' "

"That's right! Right on!" the students said, as they moved a few inches out from the walls.

"That's what we say. Because it ends up being namby-pamby, let's have this committee, that committee, the other committee," Brown concluded, laying his hands on the table.

After a brief silence, apparently feeling it his duty as Smith's new ombudsman, Pentony spoke up. "We agree. There is a necessity. But the trustees do have the power—this board is partially a Reagan-appointed board. They have the power to say, 'You guys skirted the procedures, and we veto it.' We've got a job to do," Pentony advised, "and I am willing to go down to the trustees and say, 'This is what we have to do,' and I think we have to get some political pressure from the black community to do that with the trustees."

"You establish a Black Studies Department today and every black person will be behind you," Brown replied immediately with the assurance of an expert.

The discussion continued, while the students exchanged impressions in whispers. Whenever people began to talk at once, Varnado would bang on the table and remind them that everybody couldn't talk at the same time. Just as moods were mellowing and everyone had begun to assume that there would be a department, one of the students mentioned Hare's salary. The administrators attempted to explain that department chairmen's salaries were a question of rank rather than academic position.

"Hold it, hold it," Varnado said, to stop them. "First of all, what you're saying is, Dr. Hare's salary is going to be raised. Right? Right! That's for sure. They're going to raise the salary because we decided that last night. It's just a question of how high."

Displeased, Smith asked, "You see what's happening here?"

"What's happening here?" Varnado responded defiantly.

"What's happening here is the thesis that people completely

outside of responsibility to the trustees and the state college system, outside of the specific authority of the president, are going to determine the salaries of the faculty and the administrators of the college. Now is that what you're asking us?"

Brown began to interpret Varnado's remarks. "I feel like I always have to be the contemporary historian. Let me see if I can give you some of the background. Many decisions have been made and everybody's just out there, and somebody says, 'This is going to happen, and that's going to happen,' and black people haven't had anything to do with it. The tide has turned, and black people are saying, 'We are going to determine our own destiny.' And I guess this is what they said last night. 'We determine that the brother is going to make more money, because we never had anything to do about it before and so at this point we are going to exaggerate and we are going to determine it,' so I am sure this is what he means."

"I am not giving any raise today, and that's that," Smith said, closing the issue of salary because it was not on the agenda. After a short pause, as administrators and students exchanged opinions on Hare's salary, Smith asked the group: "What I want to know is, is this kind of discussion-confrontation designed to run roughshod over all the procedures in the college, and all kinds of ways in which we are able to get long-range financial support for programs to which the college is really committed, because of a sense of urgency, or is there willingness for us to work with the cooperation of the administrative staff? Now if we try to take courses in economics and creative arts and so on out of all these departments and put them in another department and then say, 'This is Black Studies' . . . there is no tradition for that."

"This is what I am trying to say. This is the whole problem," Nathan Hare broke in, his voice trembling and angry. "Tradition is what has kept us down already. Now you are going to ask us to obey and abide by that tradition which has kept us down and kept the blacks out of the system all this time. We cannot go through the same tradition which is developed to institutionalize the suppression of blackness."

Smith attempted to save the situation. He cited examples of what his administration had done for the blacks, saying they had spent to that day more than one quarter of a million dollars for the specially admitted students. But he was cut short by the students who wanted Hare to finish. By now, they had completely surrounded the administrators and were angrily staring at the whites. Their shouts could be heard by the janitors who were cleaning up the deserted hallways of the Administration Building. Hare told the administrators that he needed salaries for six full-time professors.

As patience ran short, Reverend Williams asked that a summary of the day's efforts be drawn. He wondered if a conclusion could be made from it, and also suggested that the proposed Black Studies Department not be a "nut shell, even if in fact we had to break tradition by bringing in courses from other departments."

"I am not prepared to take a course in economics and assign it to this department on one day's notice. If that's an answer to your question, that's so," Smith said firmly, "and I am not going to order the academic vice-president to do it. So I am the problem here."

"Robert Smith," Varnado said sarcastically, "Robert Smith, you mentioned this kind of talk-confrontation and things like that. What other kind of confrontation would you rather have with us beside the talk-confrontation? First question."

It was the second time in two weeks that Varnado had threatened Smith, who feared violence would erupt on campus when the college opened for the fall semester ten days later. At a similar meting earlier, Varnado had asked, "What would you suggest we do, Dr. Smith, if everything fell through? I mean, if we didn't get one thing that we wanted. Would you suggest we rampage across the campus? Would you suggest we come and talk to you some more? What would you suggest we do?" Retaining his composure, Smith had replied, "I would certainly suggest you come and talk to us before you rampage across the campus."

Now came Varnado's second question. "One of the reasons that you don't want to ratify the program is that you want us to spend two years like white folks do researching the program and maybe get some kind of grant so we can say we spent two years trying to get a Black Studies program . . . Now there shouldn't be too much other discussion. If you're not going to support the program, you say you're not going to support it. And in that case, you don't have no more . . . you're meaningless at this meeting."

Smith didn't have an opportunity to answer.

Varnado was shaking his head and saying, "All these dogs understand what we've been talking about. They understand thoroughly. People have been going on, over and over again over the same thing. They understand. They understand fire." Varnado took a book of matches out of his pocket and lit a piece of paper that was crumbled in an ashtray on the table in front of him. He stared at it as it burned.

Threats seemed to push the two sides further apart. Now all Smith and his assistants could say was, "We can't do it." The blacks angrily retorted, "Who can do it then?" Nobody seemed to know. It was difficult to hear anything at all in the room.

Those present parted that afternoon without being able to reach an agreement, not even about the press release in which the administration announced that there was a Black Studies Department at San Francisco State College and that Nathan Hare was its acting chairman. The department had been allocated 1.3 positions, one for Hare and .3 for his part-time secretary.

In a column about a week later in the *Daily Gater,* the Black Student Union said, "In the coming semester we will be engaged in revolutionary political activity."

5

Revolutionary Political Activity

THE BLACK STUDENT LEADERS HAD NOT BEEN SURE OF EXACTLY what they meant by "revolutionary political activity" in their *Daily Gater* column of September 25, but they asked the college's more than a dozen black professors and the BSU members who were also teaching assistants to meet with them on Friday, October 11, to involve them in the "activity." At that meeting, student participants brought up the issues of the Black Studies Department, George Murray's future, and the BSU's survival as a campus organization.

Late in September, the trustees of the state college system had ordered Murray reassigned to a "nonteaching" position. Murray could not be fired without legitimate grounds during the term of his one-year contract, but the trustees preferred to pay him a salary for doing nothing rather than to have him teaching at the college. The "nonteaching" position was a fiction. The administration could not force Murray to do anything but teach.

At the meeting, BSU student leaders told the black faculty members that the trustees were also about to tighten control on the finances of student organizations. This move would be directed specifically against the BSU, the students told the older blacks, because their organization now had total control of key positions in the student government. The speaker of the legislature was a member of the BSU; the chairman of the finance committee had been handpicked by them; and, in the words of Jerry Varnado, the white officers and the majority of the legislators "had great respect" for the blacks.

After the black students at the meeting had bitterly recounted their grievances against the administration, Varnado proposed that all blacks on campus retaliate by striking on October 28. Earlier that day, he had seen the movie "The Battle of Algiers" in the company of a new member of the Central Committee, Leroy Goodwin, whose political mentor he had recently become. On their way to the meeting with the faculty, they talked about the movie, which in documentary form told the story of the Algerians' fight for independence from France. Both of them admired the Algerians' courage and determination. From this discussion, Varnado's concept of the strike emerged. The strike would serve to assess BSU strength and would help them organize the entire black student body at the college for bigger things. Nothing else Varnado had thought of was aggressive enough. He felt that it was his function as a black leader to force the Central Committee and ultimately the BSU membership to a respectably aggressive policy.

On the day of the meeting, Varnado introduced his plan, and George Murray, another close personal friend, immediately supported it. These two made it a habit to stand by each other automatically, and once they had committed themselves in the presence of the most prominent members of the college's black community, they felt that they could not back down. "We forced it on them," Varnado would recall later. But the young teachers could have won the support of the some fifteen older black faculty members on the strength of their arguments alone. Only Jack Alexis at first opposed the idea. He thought that there was not enough time to get ready for an adequate strike.

"We'd better wait until next semester. That will give us more time to prepare other campuses so that this will be a state-wide strike," he explained. Alexis argued that the BSU could also wage a more effective attack with money, and said that their chances of obtaining a grant from the Carnegie Foundation were better than the previous semester, when they had been turned down. "If we keep quiet they'll give us the money this semester," he claimed. Besides giving the black student leaders economic security, money could pay for BSU propaganda.

Unlike his associates in the BSU, Alexis believed in elaborate planning and organization. At junior college, he had established a group called United Strength, through which he had organized black and white students as tutors to underprivileged children in the San Mateo area. On the basis of this experience, he thought that the BSU could not mobilize students, particularly white ones, in only a month. Alexis was afraid that an ill-prepared effort would give the BSU adverse publicity and make them lose the grant. He told the professors and students at the meeting that he was already marshaling white faculty support for the blacks in the college's constitutional convention, which would be held later in the semester, arguing that he could easily divert that support to the strike.

The faculty Academic Senate had initiated this convention to draw up a constitution by which the college community would be governed, and Alexis claimed that, if properly approached, many among this group would side with the blacks in the coming semester, although not now. "They have their own complaints. They want to be autonomous of the trustees as much as we do," he said.

But his argument failed to convince the other students and the black faculty members, who simply did not wish to be part of Alexis' grandiose plans. The professors had come to the meeting only to avoid friction with the BSU. Alexis' student opponents thought that he was motivated by caution rather than political wisdom. Besides, they felt that he tended to fraternize too much with "white folks." Many of the BSU leaders believed that they should do without white support—mainly because whites were not reliable. They also believed that after the strike the BSU would "do something else," which it was not now necessary to specify. The planned strike would assess their strength among the black student body, but white involvement might only make some blacks turn against the BSU because potential white supporters would be from the Left. The whites' disdain of material things made some black students uncomfortable. As one of the black students said when a secretary asked if he could be reached at the Experimental College, "We don't have anything to do with those dirty hippies."

Jack Alexis took his defeat at this October meeting quietly. Rather than lose his position on the Central Committee, he agreed to work for the proposed strike. The meeting broke up after committees had been organized to announce the strike plan to the black college community and to obtain its support. The black professors were to explain the causes of the strike to the black students in their classes. Members of the Central Committee had given themselves the duty of enlisting other blacks who could not be reached through the classroom, such as employees of the college and students who were not enrolled in classes taught by black professors or black teaching assistants. Jerry Varnado, who had once belonged to the college's only Negro fraternity, the Omegas, volunteered to get their support. The task of organizing the college employees was assigned to Jack Alexis, since he was already in communication with them about the constitutional convention.

In the coming weeks, teaching assistants like Alexis would take time to discuss the proposed Black Studies Department during their classes, giving examples drawn from their summer dealings with the administration to show why a strike was necessary. Later in October, as the possibility of the trustees' firing George Murray increased, the BSU would use his case as evidence of what the administration and the trustees could do to a black professor, arguing that Murray would surely be fired eventually because he spoke out against "the pig power structure."

Although at no time during October did it become clear what the BSU intended to do after its one-day strike, student leaders continually talked over different possibilities. It was understood that they would not stop at the black walkout and that their next move would be more dramatic. No matter what each one of the Central Committee members had in mind, he could fit it in with Benny Stewart's overall plan for their "struggle." Almost a week after their first meeting, BSU leaders had met with black faculty members again, and the BSU chairman had introduced the idea of adopting the "war of the flea" as a technique in the black students' fight against the administration. Stewart had recently read descriptions of guerrilla tactics in a book by Robert Taber, entitled *The War of the Flea*, and in the words of one BSU member "he was fascinated."

During the week of October 24, the BSU leaders met for a progress report. Finding that they were far short of mobilizing the entire black college community, they postponed the strike. Now it was planned for Wednesday, November 6, which they termed "a historic day" because it was the first anniversary of the black students' attack on the white editor and staff of the student daily.

At this meeting, the BSU leaders also decided what their strike demands would be. As they discussed the demands, most of which centered on the Black Studies Department, the topic of special admittees arose. The administration had promised to admit four hundred black freshmen who under normal admission policies would not qualify. Some of the black leaders at the meeting suggested that the number of special admittees be doubled. Others wanted the number of 800 rounded to a thousand. Still others proposed 1500. As the bids were rising, George Murray interrupted. "Look here, brother," he said, "write down 'all black students who apply.'"

When the discussion turned to financial aid for these special admittees, BSU members who had had experience with the Office of Financial Aid on campus began to complain about how it was run. After very brief discussion, the group decided to adopt Murray's attitude. Instead of asking that the woman in charge of the office change her policy toward the blacks, they decided to demand that she be replaced. A week later, when Murray was finally suspended, another demand was added to the list, which already numbered nine. The tenth demand was that Murray not be fired.

At the time Murray accidentally revealed the plans for the black strike, South African singer Miriam Makeba, the wife of Stokely Carmichael, was scheduled to perform in a San Francisco hotel. One afternoon that week Jerry Varnado was in his apartment listening to new records. He enjoys showing his elaborate stereo equipment to his friends, and always points out to newcomers that it is economically sound to keep his collection of albums at less than one hundred by trading old ones in. As Varnado was putting on his newest purchase, his red telephone rang. It was a Panther friend who asked him to pick Carmichael up at the San Francisco International Airport that day. Excited at the prospect of seeing Carmichael again in such close quarters, Varnado agreed.

That afternoon, driving Carmichael to the city, Varnado explained in detail his view of what the BSU was up to. Taking advantage of his opportunity, he asked Carmichael to talk to the BSU at San Francisco State. But Carmichael said that he had decided to make fewer public appearances, and even after Varnado told him that the talk would not be publicized, did not promise to speak, but only said that he would "see." Carmichael would say later, "I hate public rallies," explaining:

"You know like you go to church on Sunday and you feel good for the bad things you did last week, but you know you're going to do them the following week anyhow. And we don't want rallies to become that, you know, that you come to the Black Student Union meeting . . . because you were trying to be white last week and you're going to go out and be white next week." That night, Varnado proudly told his associates on the Central Committee about his encounter with Stokely, and that the young black hero had promised to speak to the BSU.

On the afternoon of Sunday, November 3, the Central Committee met at the San Francisco Black Panther party headquarters to prepare the announcement of their strike. They had scheduled a press conference for the following day, November 4, when the announcement was to be made.

On that morning around eleven o'clock, a group of blacks walked into the Gallery Lounge, where students were listening to the radio, playing chess on the worn set which belongs to the Associated Students, or reading the newspaper. Newsmen were also in the lounge. A heavy-set black student, after summoning two companions and giving instructions in a low voice, walked to the middle of the room, his unbuttoned, three-quarter-length black leather jacket flapping on his thighs. In formal tones, he announced: "We're going to hold a press conference here. If you don't have a press pass, leave." Most students left without objection, and he walked about to examine the credentials of those who remained, some of whom were escorted from the lounge by a waiting group of blacks. When the room had been cleared of everyone but the press, two black students posted themselves at the exits.

Soon a new group of black students arrived. They talked for a few minutes, and then pulled a couch, and two chairs to the south corner. On the bulletin board which usually held student paintings and photographs, they posted pictures of Huey Newton, Eldridge Cleaver, and an issue of that day's *Gater*, which had a picture of George Murray on its front page. While other radio and television reporters were arriving, the same students pulled up a coffee table and placed it in front of the couch. A bank of microphones soon covered the table. Cameramen exchanged jokes as they unwound their gear and plugged their light fixtures into the socket behind the couch. By now, the impatient newsmen were checking the time—the press conference was already fifteen minutes late. Then Varnado, Stewart, and other members of the BSU entered the room, accompanied by Nathan Hare and Joseph White, the latter one of the four black administrators of the college.

The black students, who by now numbered one hundred, and the fifteen newsmen gradually grew silent. Occasional remarks by the journalists seemed loud because it was so quiet. Varnado, Stewart, Hare, and White sat on the couch. A few of the less well-known members of the Central Committee stood behind it. Hare and White, who represented the faculty and the administration respectively, had come to the press conference to emphasize the fact that all the blacks at the college would be going on strike. Stewart, who that day wore a black beret and a blue Nehru jacket, turned around. Peering through his blue tinted glasses, he said, "We want more black people around us to show on television," seemingly in response to the contention that only a small number of black students were behind the strike. At his words, some of the black students who were watching tapped the cameramen on the shoulders, passed by them, and moved forward to go behind the couch.

"That's much better," Stewart said quietly. Then, raising his voice, he exclaimed, "Power to the people."

Here and there, timid voices replied, "Power to the people."

Stewart smiled at the shy response, and shook his head like an experienced craftsman teaching his skill.

"No, no," he said, "nobody heard you. Let's try it again."

"All power to the people. Black power to the black people,"

the BSU chairman chanted. Unlike other BSU leaders, Stewart took public chanting seriously, and he wanted the black "revolutionary" mood to be clear.

Stewart had once been deeply religious, a member of the Pentecostal Church of Christ and God, which draws its congregation, he says, from "the lumpen proletariat, the lower classes" of the black community. At that time, he believed that black America's wounds could be healed only in the church. Quiet and withdrawn when he entered San Francisco State in 1966, he was now known as a fiercely vocal militant, businesslike in manner. He had joined the black student organization that year, after seeing its members challenge white Ph.D.s. Stewart had come to believe that he should be helping his people to improve their lives on earth rather than to prepare for some future life, as the church taught. Sincere and dedicated, he was now committed to the BSU, and through the personal intervention of Garrett, former chairman and architect of the organization, he had succeeded to the chair. In due time, Stewart's friends revealed that Garrett had made him chairman only to use him. When Stewart realized that they were right, he became harsher and more dogmatic.

On the day of the press conference, he stood back waiting quietly for a more energetic reply from BSU members.

"Power to the people," repeated the black students, this time more confidently.

"Black power to the black people," they continued, even more loudly.

Satisfied, Stewart picked up the dittoed press statement from the coffee table in front of him and began to read.

> Black people, including students, staff workers, teachers, and administrators will be striking on November 6. We are striking to focus national and international attention on our situation at this campus. It is also a method to teach and educate others about our struggle. We intend to determine our own destiny as true men and women. Brother Malcolm

X, by his courageous life and character, laid the foundation for the struggle of black people for their liberation. Brother Huey Newton demonstrated the importance of black men to act as a force on principle against the white oppressor. Since black people will determine their destiny not only here but across this nation, we must act against the white oppressor and invoke the political consequences when our rights are violated.

As soon as he had finished reading, the eager newsmen vied with each other to make their questions heard. Stewart ignored them. He picked up another sheet of paper from the table and began to enumerate the BSU's demands, ten altogether. Among them were a demand that the Black Studies Department be allowed to grant the B.A. degree, that George Murray be reinstated, and that Nathan Hare receive a salary suitable to his qualifications. The following day, Stewart would explain, "You've got some dumbfounded, silly-assed racist [chairman] making at least $18,000 a year, and you've got Nathan Hare, about the heaviest black sociologist in this country, receiving half a professorship." Now Stewart proudly introduced the sociologist, saying that Dr. Hare would explain the status of the Black Studies Department.

"The department is a paper department," Hare began. He sat on the edge of the couch, which could not seat four comfortably. Leaning forward, he went on, "We have no courses, no faculty. We are not assigned to a school." Since the college's more than sixty departments are distributed among five schools, it seemed to Hare that this was a sign that the administration did not intend his department to be permanent.

"It's a polka-dot studies [department]," he explained. "The whites are trying to force on us what the nature of our department should be."

Members of the press only asked the inevitable question: "What do the black students intend to do on November 6?"

"Whites have a lot of gall, asking us what we are going to

do," Hare snapped back, shaking his head in disbelief. The students behind him supported him with hearty cries. When reporters asked questions on tactics, no one answered. Then the newsmen, believing that the strike was a direct consequence of Murray's suspension, asked if it were significant that the demand for the Black Panther's reinstatement was listed last.

"All the demands have the same priority," replied Jerry Varnado, who had been sitting silently, his Zapata mustache accentuating his grimace.

"We won't compromise on any of them," he said.

After the ouster of Jimmy Garrett, the former chairman, BSU members had become very careful not to allow one person to emerge as dominant. To ensure a collective leadership, they had established the Central Committee, which was elected by the membership. Under the new system, it was agreed, recurrence of past manipulation of members by a single figure could not occur. Although not all members of the Central Committee wielded equal power at the time of the press conference, the group was attempting to project an image of total equality by having all its members present and letting more than one person speak. The fact that Varnado had become the most powerful member of the Central Committee was attributed by some to his personality. He saw no middle ground on any issue. Having classified someone as an enemy or a friend, he refused to admit into discussion any evidence which contradicted his opinion.

About seven o'clock on the morning of November 5, Varnado and Jack Alexis left the apartment they then shared on Steiner Street off Page, in a neighborhood which Varnado proudly says is in the heart of the black Fillmore district. Crossing the street, the two entered the building opposite theirs. Soon other BSU leaders joined them in the apartment of the Black Panther's national Field Marshal, Donald Cox. If for no other reason than that he lived close to the students, he had kept in touch with them. At the insistence of BSU leaders,

D. C. had arranged for Stokely Carmichael to speak at the college on the eve of the strike. Carmichael had asked to meet with the students that morning to ask questions about their plans. They in turn were to get advice from him. Early that morning, D. C. had gone to pick Carmichael up at a hospital where his wife was being treated. Carmichael seemed tired and depressed, so the students avoided unnecessary questions and tried to make their replies to his inquiries brief. They believed that the former chairman of the Student Non-Violent Coordinating Committee had been reluctant to address their organization because he saw little significance in the BSU's fight at San Francisco State. When they explained to him that they did not plan to end their militant activities after the one-day strike, it seemed to the students that Carmichael was pleased, especially with Stewart's planning of the "war of the flea." The students also told Carmichael that the primary purpose of the strike was to assess their strength and that his appearance would help to increase their support on campus.

Shortly before eight o'clock, the meeting broke up and the students went on to San Francisco State. There, Alexis opened the BSU office, of which he was in charge, and prepared leaflets for the afternoon speech. Alexis took his work seriously, and he tried to make the BSU office a center for blacks on campus. He had established rules to ensure respectability for their headquarters. One of his rules which almost everyone agreed upon prohibited eating meals in the office. Although everyone respected this rule, Varnado occasionally sent a BSU member to buy his lunch in the cafeteria because he wanted to avoid eating in a room filled with whites. But every time he broke the rule, Alexis argued with him bitterly.

By mid-morning, Alexis had the leaflets ready to be handed to the BSU members who would distribute them among black students and post them in the vicinity of the cafeteria.

That afternoon, as black students were crowding into the Main Auditorium, where Carmichael was to speak, a long-haired white student entered the lobby. As he approached the main entrance to the auditorium, one of the two female BSU members who were acting as ushers told him sternly that the meeting was open only to black and Third World students. Shrugging his shoulders and smiling faintly, the long-haired young man strolled out with a bouncing walk. Entrance was also refused other white students who had come to hear Carmichael. According to the college bylaws governing student activities, no meeting could be closed to students on the basis of their race. But the administration had ignored such practices over the past two years, hoping that they were temporary.

The 700 seats in the auditorium were soon filled, and a few students stood in the aisles. On this rare occasion, almost all the estimated 800 black students at San Francisco State had come to see the black hero. Individual chatter in the auditorium changed to wild applause when Carmichael appeared, accompanied by Varnado, Stewart, and several young Panther bodyguards. Their eyes shining with enthusiasm, the students stood up to clap fast and steadily. As the applause began to die, Stewart quickly introduced the main speaker of the day. Carmichael was greeted again by another round of applause, this time accompanied by cheers and laughter. He approached the podium, wearing a dashiki and dark glasses. He pressed the palms of his hands on the podium, and began to speak.

"I didn't really intend to speak today, for a number of reasons," he said, "but before I go into that, I want to tell you about the importance of a man like Dr. Hare."

Nathan Hare was sitting motionless behind Carmichael on the stage with three members of the Central Committee, his arms folded across his chest, his legs crossed.

"The importance of Dr. Hare is that he taught me an attitude. Because he did teach me when I was at Howard. But he didn't teach me sociology, because anybody can teach you sociology. The importance of Dr. Hare is that he taught me an attitude," Carmichael repeated. "And it's the attitude that he

has that is more important than the specific technical material
that he can give you in the classroom, and I think that you
have to begin to understand that if we're seriously going to talk
about challenging education around this country today.

"Let me give you some examples," he went on. "We all had
reading comprehension. Somebody used to let us read it and
then answer questions, and we would read it and try to be
smart. But now you have to understand what the attitude was.
We read something. We read, for example: Abraham Lincoln
was a poor boy, born in a log cabin, who worked very hard; he
was very honest, he read a lot, he studied well, and therefore he
became President of the United States. And the question they
asked you was, 'How did he become President of the United
States?' We thought we were exercising our brains, but what
we were doing was"—Carmichael made his voice quieter with
every word—"being whitewashed, whitewashed, whitewashed
. . . over and over again."

All the 700 students in the audience listened carefully, except for the male ushers who were also serving as guards. Now
stationed along the walls of the auditorium, they were not listening to Carmichael but watching the audience closely in case
someone tried to attack him.

He was explaining, "Now the attitude of white America is
that you must be responsible, you must love, worship, be patri-
otic, etc., etc., to them. The attitude of us must be"—he
paused between each word—"that we must oppose white
America on every level. On every ground we must oppose
them." Now Carmichael began to talk at a more normal rate.
"How do black students begin to move to do that? Some of
these things we can talk about very briefly . . . no entertainment today."

He went on in smooth, velvety tones: "Then you must be
able to sustain the struggle. Now how do you sustain the struggle? You sustain the struggle by first deciding what your aims
and goals are. And you decide that nothing can stop you from

achieving those aims and those goals. Once you have decided that, you're ready for the struggle. For example," he said, lifting his palms from the podium and shifting his weight, "let us joke."

"You come on campus, and you decide you're going to get on a sister. No matter what, if it's going to take you the entire semester, you're going to get the sister. You don't stop until you get her. Nothing stops you . . ."

Now the audience was laughing. Soon they began to applaud.

"Nothing at all," Carmichael went on, when it was quiet again. "We must have the same type of attitude in a more serious matter, about our struggle. So that we cannot any longer just throw out phrases: we want freedom, we want self-determination, we want this. Everybody wants that. If we say the same thing that Lyndon Johnson is saying, then there is something wrong with us." There were a few cries of "Right on" from different sections of the auditorium. "If we're going to sustain our struggle," Carmichael continued, "we must give to our people something specific that they can work on, but always in terms of the attitude because that's far more important than the specific. That sounds confusing, but let me go on with it.

"For example, if the Black Student Union says, 'We want this white person kicked out, we want them replaced with a black person,' that's not enough. It's not enough because they can replace them with any black person. Now the way to insure that you get somebody who is to your liking, who is someone who will do what you want them to do, who has the same political ideology that you have, is to make sure that you can choose or you have control over that person. And that's far more important than the specific person.

"Black people get up today and say, 'We are black and we want a black so-and-so,' and they give you a black so-and-so." A few students burst into giggles. "A man who listens to the white power structure," Carmichael explained. Then there was general applause. "That's visible power."

"We must go now for the real control. We must go now for the *real* control. That's got to be the word, the real control. We want the power to pick, to hire, and to fire. That's the attitude." He leaned forward.

"Now I want to explain the general and the specific. All of you have, or will have, logic. You know how logic works. You start off with a general assumption. It is the attitude and the general that we want. We want the right to hire and to fire teachers. We want the right to control the Black Student Union courses at San Francisco State, and once we get that then George Murray becomes irrelevant. Because George Murray is under our control, and Mayor Alioto has nothing to say about it. But if we fight over George Murray, even if we win next week, then they'll pick somebody else."

Carmichael stopped for a moment. "I know this is boring because it's not entertainment," he said. "But it's far more important, far more important." He stopped again.

"We have to begin to understand these things. Now," he said in a lower tone, wiping the sweat from his forehead, "the Black Student Union at San Francisco State is the most notorious in the country . . ." The excited students interrupted him with frenzied applause. The BSU's aggressive stance during recent years and the power they had secured at the college had made them self-conscious. Carmichael now talked slowly and carefully: "I think that's good. I hope you do not think it's good. Because if you think it's good, then you're in trouble. Because if you think it's good you might let notoriety become your goal. It should not become your goal. If it happens to be incidentally you are the most notorious, then that's good. But if it became your goal and end that you want to be the most notorious, you're in trouble, you're in trouble."

Unhappy about the BSU's image and privately accusing their leaders of showing off, a small faction of the audience heard these remarks with approval. They began to applaud. Because it was Stokely who was being critical, the entire audience joined in.

"I believe that's the attitude you must aim for," Carmichael went on. "If you do it, you do a lot of favors. If you can set the attitude at San Francisco State, you will be duplicated across this country overnight. Overnight it will be duplicated. It will save us a lot of trouble just running around telling each Black Student Union what to do—and there are thousands of them in this country. Because you will already have done it. You will have elevated the struggle from the specific to the general. But now sustaining the struggle is what's important. You should not start off doing activities which you cannot maintain or sustain over a prolonged period of time. You should not do that. If you can only start off with one step a day, one picket sign a day, then if that picket sign can go on for a prolonged period of time, you do that, you do that. But do not start off with something you cannot maintain because in the long run you not only hurt yourself but movements to come.

"More importantly, you delude yourself and delude the entire black community. Because you assume that the fight you're fighting is an easy fight and it will be all over tomorrow. That's not true. Our fight is a fight of this entire generation. The entire generation! The entire generation has to give its talent, its skill, its sweat and blood and its life to the struggle," Carmichael said.

After stressing the importance of the black students' strike, he warned them against depending on whites. "Look to make allies among those people who suffer like you do. That's black people. And then there's people of color.

"And the war is going to be waged on different levels, but for college students mainly it's going to be waged on the psychological level. Your biggest fight will be television. That's a fact. You underestimate it, but your biggest fight will be television. Because Mayor Alioto can call a press conference anytime he wants to and put on any program he wants and can bring any Negro he wants to fight you on television."

Carmichael said that since the blacks don't control television, they have to pick their own "arena" after they have made "a clear analysis" of where they are going. "We do not regress," he explained, "we always *progress*. There have been buildings seized before. You've done it here last year. Big deal! To come back and seize it again doesn't excite anybody. Victory is what we want, not notoriety.

"You may start something that you may not even finish at San Francisco State. Maybe the freshmen who come after you will have to pick up, but if the struggle is correct they will be able to fit in immediately and will not have to go over the problems you had when you first came here: should I join the Black Student Union? should I wear a natural? All of those personal problems will become irrelevant if you set the correct attitude. In order to do that, we must have a clear definition of what our problems are.

"[Students] think that merely adding Swahili instead of French makes something black. That's ridiculous! When you talk about black studies, you talk about methodology and ideology, not just another subject. Methodology and ideology.

"So that when we talk about methodology, we talk about different methods of even communicating. Let me give you an example. All the speeches that black people have made across this country, Rap Brown, Huey P. Newton, Eldridge Cleaver, Bobby Seale, Ron Karenga, Leroi Jones, James Farmer, James Forman, everybody, was not as significant as one single act," Carmichael said, raising his right hand in a clenched fist. At the sight of the Panther salute, the audience applauded wildly. He was referring to the Panther athletes' salute at the 1968 Olympics in Mexico.

"That one act communicated to all of us, and we knew precisely what it said," he explained. "It's a different methodology. And then if we talk about Black Studies, we talk about different methodology, not the same methodology the white man uses.

"Secondly, ideology. All of the courses we read are riddled with white racism. Different ideology means ideology rooted in black nationalism, not just adding black people to white history. That's a subterfuge. It's an insidious subterfuge," he said, raising his voice in anger. "It is going to misdirect our struggle if we allow that to happen. Because finally we have to—and it's your job—to heighten the contradictions while we prepare for the confrontation. I want to repeat that, because it's vitally important. We must heighten the contradiction as we prepare for the confrontation. Too many people seek to heighten the confrontation and don't understand the contradictions. We cannot heighten the confrontation. We must heighten the contradictions. While we heighten the contradictions, we politically awake our people, we make them become more politically aware. Then we prepare for the confrontation so that when the confrontation does come we"—he stopped—"become victorious. It is easy to die for one's people." He stopped and then went on in a lower, even tone. "It is much more difficult to live, to work, and to kill for one's people."

The steady hand-clapping grew louder and louder. The audience stood up. When the applause died down, Carmichael warned the students again about the danger of heightening the confrontation without first heightening the contradictions. Then he concluded his speech in quiet and grave tones: "It is easier to die for one's people than it is to work and live for them, to kill for them, and to continue to live and kill for them. Thank you."

The students stood up again and applauded continuously.

This was Carmichael's second appearance at San Francisco State. Both times, the young black leader had received an unusually warm welcome. The first time, he had read a paper later to be published in the *Massachusetts Review*. On that occasion, the audience had been racially mixed, but the first few rows of seats were reserved for blacks.

"Hold on. It's not over yet. Everybody sit down." Chairman Benny Stewart was addressing students who had rushed to the exits in hopes of getting out before the crowd.

"I take it for granted that you didn't know the meeting was not over yet," he said. "Because, otherwise, you're doing just what Stokely said, like people who come for the soul-searching, feel-good meeting and run off when we're going to take care of business. Brother Carmichael said some very beautiful things about the prolonged struggle." It seemed that Stewart was trying to emphasize the importance of what he had to say by talking slowly.

"It just so happens that the members of the BSU Central Committee have been analyzing how student movements have been functioning, taking over for two or three days and then the thing is dead. From our analysis, we think that we have developed a technique to deal with this for a prolonged struggle. We call it the war of the flea, the war of a flea. What does a flea do? Bites, sucks blood from the dog. The dog bites. And what happens when there's enough fleas on the dog? What will he do? He moves, he moves away, he moves on." Stewart paused, as if he wanted to make sure the audience had time to take in what he was saying.

"And what the Man has been running down on us, he psychs us out in terms of our manhood. He'll say, 'What you goin' do, Nigger? You're trying to be a man?' Here he is with shotgun, billy clubs, .357 magnum. All you got is heart.

"That's not the way it's going no more. We are the people. We are the majority, and the pigs"—he drew the word out— "cannot be everywhere, everyplace, all the time. Where they are not, we get on. And something happens." He paused.

"The philosophy of the flea. It just begins to"—he stopped at every word—"wear them down. Something is always calling them. If you can dig it? I talked to some of the students in my class"—he paused again—"and it heightens all the time. Toilets are stuffed up, water in the bathroom is just running all over the place, smoke is coming out of the bathroom. 'I don't know nothing about it. I'm on my way to take an exam. Don't look at me! Man, would I burn up a bathroom? Me?' And when the pigs come down in full force, ain't nothing happen. You retreat, and when they split, it goes on"—he accentuated each word—"and on and on. Tomorrow we'll talk more about the flea, develop it some more. I've spoken already to various people about the flea because this is our power.

"We will fight the racist administration on our grounds from now on, where we can win. When he disrespects our humanity, then he pays. That's it! He has to be educated to our Friday and Saturday night philosophy. 'Look you stepped on my shoes.' 'Don't worry about that.' Whop." Stewart said it with a slapping gesture. " 'Didn't I tell you to stop talkin' to my woman?' Whop!" The audience giggled.

Stewart then recounted a conversation he had had earlier that day with a young "brother" who had cautioned him to "act nice" because he was in a minority.

"I listened to what he was saying and I told him to have a seat because I wanted to talk to him. And it just so happens that there was a brother that was much bigger than he was and I asked him, I said, 'What would you do if that brother come in with some lipstick and just chalked it all over your jacket?' 'Man,' he said, 'I'd cut that motherfucker's ass!' I said, 'Hold on, brother, you can't do that. He's bigger than you.' He said, 'Don't make no difference!' " Steward went on, imitating an angry young black.

"But it's the principle, see?" he continued. "We're in a minority here. We can't do this; we can't do that. The other thing I asked him: 'All right we're out here on this college campus, struggling for our humanity. Does that mean that since we're out here on this college campus that a white boy can walk up to you and slap you down, or if you're at Macy's or the Emporium they can slap you down? No, it don't work like that. Your manhood, your respect, your dignity, you don't leave it at home when you walk off and catch a bus. It goes everywhere with you. That's the principle.' Then that brother could begin to see what's got to come down."

Stewart's anecdote had defined the BSU's militant stance for the audience.

"And it just so happens," he continued, "that when we spoke to Stokely earlier today concerning tactics, we was thinking right along the same levels.

"If we're not ready to back up no principle, then we can forget it. You can go back to playing. What kind of a man is a man that is going to allow some dude to kick him in his ass and slap him around all the time? How can we respect this person as being a man? He has got to back up the principle, and the tactic that has to be employed has to be that of the flea. It's here and there. Constantly wearing down, not in large masses, but two's, three's, and four's. Constantly!

"This is what it's got to come down to. If we're serious, then we can do it. We can do it. The most important thing is that it can be done and escape the wrath of the oppressor. We watch all these James Bond flicks, Sherlock Holmes. White man always gets his man. But we want to do away with that mess.

"We want to see action going down, people going to class, and getting with that exam. And boom. You walk out. 'Man, what happened? Who would do something like that?' Right in the middle of exams, boom, that's it. And some of these racist pigs who's on the Academic Senate who thinks they are beyond the wrath of the people, they have to be educated too, you see. Because sometimes when they jump in their Mercedes-Benzes, it ain't goin' to start up all the time. If you dig it? And then they begin to learn that they are not beyond the reaches of the people. And then they won't be so cold. But later on we should move to control them, to consolidate. We must gain grounds to consolidate controls, and that is the way that we have to be thinking. So once we control the area, don't worry about it anymore. We're moving on."

Stewart concluded his remarks that day by inviting the audience to meet again the next day around eleven o'clock to talk "some more about the war of the flea."

6

The Strike Begins

WEDNESDAY, NOVEMBER 6, WAS A COLD, RAINY DAY. THE area in front of the Commons was quiet, and the students standing about there were uneasy. Everyone knew that the blacks had planned a strike, which was supported by the Students for a Democratic Society. Members of the administration, expecting the worst, wished the day already over. The more liberal faculty members were waiting to see if their premonitions would prove accurate. Their conservative counterparts went about their business, as if this were just another day.

Shortly after eleven A.M., the black students met in the Main Auditorium in a mood of uncertainty. After calling the meeting to order, Benny Stewart began to repeat what he had said the previous day when he addressed the BSU meeting after Stokely Carmichael. Stewart was describing "the war of the flea" again, when a short, bearded man in the audience stood up.

"Look, man," he said abruptly, "everyone knows that. We didn't come here to talk. Let's get down to business. If we're going to go out on strike today, everybody else should be out, too."

"Right on!" many voices agreed. "Right on!"

Taken aback by this interruption, Stewart stood silently; he regained his composure and assessed the mood of the crowd before he began to talk again. This time he said what everyone in the audience wanted to hear.

"All right, then, we'll close the school down." Flipping the tip of his nose with his index finger, in his usual nervous gesture, Stewart went on: "We'll break up into groups and go into the buildings."

That day there were fewer students in the auditorium than the day before, when 700—almost the entire black student body of the college—had assembled. Stokely Carmichael had drawn this large number, but today cautious black students, who did not welcome Benny Stewart's proposed war of the flea, had stayed away from campus. After naming leaders for the proposed groups, Stewart invited the audience, in small numbers, to meet behind the stage because he didn't want to discuss in public the specific activities he had planned for that day. As the students talked to each other about their own plans for closing down the campus, the noise in the auditorium increased.

In less than half an hour, groups of ten to fifteen had been organized. Each was to take on a section in the buildings of the college where classes were being held, in order to conduct "teach-ins." Normal classroom activity was to be halted, by violence if necessary.

The students left the Main Auditorium far more confident than they had arrived, talking about the duties they had been assigned. The most belligerent among them had been sent to buildings which housed the "most reactionary and racist departments." One of the more moderate groups headed toward the Education Building. Someone suggested there that they go to the second floor where he had a class scheduled at that time. Talking loudly, their heads erect and shoulders straight, they walked up the only winding staircase on campus, making no effort to make room for students who were coming down. When he arrived at the door of the classroom, the student who had suggested that they go there hesitated a few seconds, but then opened the door and entered. The group followed. Inside, the surprised professor halted his lecture. Rather timidly, the striking student explained that the blacks were on strike because the administration had refused to establish a real Department of Black Studies.

"Do you support us?" a black girl standing in front of the class asked the professor, throwing back her head defiantly.

As the professor began to explain that he did, but that this was hardly the way to settle their grievances, another black student demanded, "Why aren't you on strike?"

"Because they're racists," another member of the invading group said, "that's why."

"I think you should dismiss the class," said another black student.

"Yeah," said his companions.

The embarrassed students in the class sat silent. Some of them moved uneasily in their seats. Others remained motionless, waiting to see what the professor would do. Aware of the rising tension, he forced a smile, picked up his notes, told the students that the class was dismissed, and quietly left the room. His students followed him slowly.

With cheers, the black students went on to another class. Here, one of them went straight to the blackboard. Picking up a piece of chalk, he wrote in capital letters: THIS CLASS IS DISMISSED. As his companions explained their actions, the professor and his students left the classroom.

But not all classes were broken up easily. As the group invaded one classroom, an angry white student, his cheeks blazing, told the blacks that he did not wish to participate in the strike. "This is my right, and I would like to exercise it," he said firmly.

"Then you're a racist," snapped a black student.

"That ain't nothing new," one of the black girls commented, as two of her friends approached the white student menacingly. In an effort to ward off a fight, the instructor tersely announced that the class was dismissed and that they would meet the next time as scheduled.

A group of about thirty black students burst into the Business and Social Sciences Building. After brief deliberation, they broke up into two groups, one to take on the ground floor, the other to go upstairs. They anticipated resistance, but they were determined to disrupt normal activities. Those on the ground floor entered an office first, where frightened secretaries watched them throwing papers, books, and pencils to the floor. Their spokesman meanwhile tapped his fingers on a desk, asking the secretaries why they were not out on strike in support of the BSU. As he was talking, another student lifted a typewriter and threw it out of the window behind him.

During these invasions, President Robert Smith's secretary kept assuring alarmed callers from all over campus that the president was doing his best to cope with the crisis. Many were calling to report fires and fist fights, and "roving bands of black students beating up whites." As his secretary and his assistants were answering the phone, Robert Smith responded to a scream of "fire" from the women's restroom. He ran out of his office and down the hall, grabbed a fire extinguisher and entered the smoky room to spray the waste basket. When he returned to his office, he learned that some 500 students were marching on the Administration Building.

The white students, unaware that these raids were taking place, had been holding a rally to denounce the administration. After the speeches, they had decided to march on the Administration Building to present Robert Smith with the strike demands.

Fearing that they might refuse to leave the building, once they entered, Smith went out immediately. He stood on the steps, stern and preoccupied, and, as soon as he could be heard, told the crowd: "There are many important things happening on campus today, and I have no time to talk to you at length. This is not the time or the place to discuss the issues that concern you." Amidst scattered boo's, he reentered the building, now guarded by the campus police. In his office, he found that the number of complaints had increased. He then ordered the campus closed, as he would say later that afternoon at a press conference, "to protect the safety of people from frightening acts and disruption," and asked the San Francisco Police Department to intervene. By 1:35, the Tactical Squad had arrived on campus and closed all the buildings, including the Gallery Lounge. White students who had taken shelter there from the rain slowly left the lounge with mutters of "Pigs." The black students had already left by then. The BSU had arranged for them to meet at their downtown, off-campus headquarters after the teach-ins.

It was still raining when the first black students arrived at the flat in a dilapidated dwelling in the middle of the Fillmore ghetto, which the BSU had rented almost a year earlier for its expanding off-campus activities. The tutorial program had grown to include nearly 500 black children. The off-campus center served also as a meeting place for aspiring young black poets and playwrights, who read their work during BSU meetings, and for discussion of politics and social issues. Black students could also meet socially there, with a record player providing background music.

This afternoon, in preparation for the BSU gathering, the stereo was at its highest volume. As the black students arrived from campus in groups of three and four, they greeted each other with their usual hand-slap salute. Some began to dance, while others talked over the day on campus, laughing. Those who had "roughed up" white students compared their experiences.

The center was now crowded with black students from the college. Nostalgically reminiscing about that afternoon of November 6, one of them, Leroi Goodwin, would say later, "It was a beautiful sight. We were all there together. The petty bourgeoisie, the lower classes. There were students from all segments of the black community." Amidst laughter and music, the students unanimously voted to return the following day to "the Freak Factory" to close it down. They referred to San Francisco State College as "the Freak Factory" because it seemed to them that it turned out petty bureaucrats or "freaks" for the Establishment of the State of California.

Later that afternoon, they broke up into several groups and continued their celebration of the day's victory in their homes. Members of the Central Committee met shortly before six o'clock at Jerry Varnado's apartment. They watched TV, rolling one "joint" after another. As the local newscasters reported on San Francisco State, the black students grew hilarious at the news that "roving bands of blacks" had beaten up white students. Later on, when everyone was leaving, Jack Alexis reminded his friends that it was important to keep the white students' support.

The next morning, white student radicals, unsure of what activities to plan for the day, scheduled a rally. The high point of the gathering came when black author John O. Killens, who had been booked several weeks earlier as a speaker in the College Lecture Series, spoke in the open air, under a warm sun, instead of in the Main Auditorium. After white secretary Sophia D'Angeli had argued that speaking inside would be interpreted by the public as not honoring the student strike, the location of the speech had been changed. Besides, there were no more than twenty students in the auditorium to hear it. Although Killen's prepared talk had nothing to do with the strike, he did relate his remarks on the role of the black writer in America to events on campus, telling an enthusiastic, racially mixed audience spread across the central lawn eating their lunches that the strike was a fight for the right of "self-determination." He called on black writers to glorify such "freedom fights," among which he also included revolts in Harlem, Detroit, and Watts.

While the rally was going on, the war of the flea continued. Petty acts of vandalism took place in different campus buildings. Toilets were clogged. Many small fires were set, one of them in the station wagon belonging to a local TV station, reputedly conservative. In reaction, Robert Smith summoned a few outside policemen whenever he felt it necessary. A Nigerian student, Paul N. Okpokam, was arrested when a homemade bomb was found in his possession.

At the conclusion of the rally, as the black students withdrew from campus, white students marched on the buildings and filed through empty corridors shouting, "On strike, shut it down," a chant which would become the slogan of the strike.

Press and television commentators interpreted this as an unsuccessful day for the striking black students. The college had not been declared officially closed, and the presence of the police on campus had gone unnoticed. The Public Information Office's estimate of nonstriking students made it seem that classes had continued almost normally.

That day other organizations had announced that they were supporting the strike. One of them was the Third World Liberation Front or TWLF, which had been organized by the black student leaders in early March of that year as a front for the BSU.

On the morning of March 5, 1968, representatives of the college's minority student organizations, comprised of Latin, Chinese, and Filipino-American groups, had been invited by the BSU's Jimmy Garrett to meet with representatives of his own organization to form a coalition. Garrett had already spoken about his plans to a Chicano, or Mexican-American, professor, Juan Martinez, who welcomed the opportunity to make new allies. Martinez at the time was fighting to remain at San Francisco State after his one-year contract had not been renewed. He had come to the college from Arizona, where he had taught history for nine years in an atmosphere he found "stifling." Now, after unsuccessfully attempting to gain support from the moderate wing of the faculty, he had turned to white radical and minority students as a last resort.

Martinez sat on the edge of his desk, feet dangling a few inches from the floor, in the long, narrow office which he shared with three other professors. He examined his wristwatch. The black delegation was late. The representative of the Intercollegiate Chinese Student Association, a young girl, sat demurely, having said earlier that she was only an observer. At the time, her organization was composed of fifty members who had not shown any interest in campus politics. Three representatives were also present from Latin American Student Organization, a group which drew its membership primarily from foreign nationals. The three were not officially representing their organization, which was mainly a social group. They were attending this meeting because of their friendship with Martinez. Also in the room was a member of the Filipino-American organization, whose membership did not exceed ten. Like the others, he had come to the meeting primarily because he personally was interested in the problems of people of color. There were also some whites present, including a *Gater* editor. Shortly before noon, several black students entered. After everyone had found a place to sit or stand, and a girl in the BSU delegation had taken out her stenographer's pad, Martinez began to talk about recruiting minority students and about the need for a coalition among the members of the Third World. Having made this introduction, Martinez stopped, waiting for comments.

At first, Jimmy Garrett seemed to be waiting for someone else to speak, but he eventually broke the silence himself to talk about the "concept of the Third World." He hadn't gone very far when one of his companions interrupted. "All you white people should get out so we can get down to business," he said. "You don't belong here anyway."

The non-black students of color were embarrassed enough at this aggressive move to intervene timidly on behalf of the few whites present. "Let them stay," the Filipino student suggested politely. "They're entitled to hear."

Sensing the mood of the non-black delegates and fearing that they might be alienated by such open hostility toward whites, Garrett said, "We spent half of last semester arguing over who are good white folks and who are bad white folks. That shit takes too much time. We got to get down to business. What about a name? Somebody suggest a name for the organization."

The students began to offer names, nearly all of which included the words "minority" and either "coalition" or "alliance."

"We've got to stop calling ourselves the minority. That's a psychological trick the Man uses. We are not the minority. He is the minority. Three-fourths of the world is non-white. We are all part of the Third World." Garrett spoke slowly, as if he were lecturing. Then he sat silently, waiting to hear other suggestions.

New names were proposed, those like "Minority Student Alliance" being rephrased "Third World Student Alliance."

"How about Third World Liberation Front?" Garrett asked. "That word 'liberation' scares him, like the brothers in Viet Nam." The group seemed pleased.

"Shall we take a vote on the names?" he asked, motioning to the black secretary to read the suggestions.

"Let's take a vote on the white boys," shouted the black student who was still preoccupied with ridding the meeting of whites.

The gathered students unanimously voted in favor of naming their alliance the Third World Liberation Front, the first such group in the nation. That semester the BSU made the name well-known, and soon many TWLF chapters began to appear on campuses all over the country. New students at San Francisco State who claimed Third World origins joined the organization and began to feel that they shared the BSU's prestige on campus.

On November 7, in the next semester, the second day of the strike, the BSU arranged a TWLF press conference in order to add five more demands to their list of ten and to have the new organization back up the black strike. Unlike Garrett, not all the members of the BSU saw the alliance with other peoples of color as merely a wise political move on the part of the blacks. Those like George Murray believed that the alliance was a meaningful step forward for all the peoples of color.

After a relatively uneventful Thursday, November 7, the Central Committee decided to escalate its tactics on the following day by more and better-planned guerrilla sorties. Benny Stewart, who by now had assumed total responsibility for coordinating the attacks, contacted active members of the BSU whom he considered trustworthy. Stewart took his task with utter seriousness, as he planned the next day's raids with his recruits. Telling them to wear stocking masks to avoid identification, he explained that sentinels with walkie-talkies would warn them if the "enemy" approached and that getaway cars would be waiting.

The black student groups began their attacks around noon. Five masked students invaded the Chemistry Department office. As frightened secretaries looked on, they overturned desks and filing cabinets. After inflicting what they thought was enough damage, they fled through the nearest exit out to the street where a car was waiting for them. An attack on the

Anthropology Department office was not as successful. There a lone secretary, who said she sympathized with the black students, told the raiders indignantly that their actions were wrong. The blacks soon panicked and fled, in fear that the crash of a window they had broken would attract attention. One determined black girl decided to inflict more damage on the office before leaving. In haste, she picked up a pair of scissors and cut the wires of an electric typewriter which had not been turned off. The electric shock threw her to the floor, where she was lying when the police arrived. One of the black males who was in the vicinity waiting for her was also arrested. The others escaped to the getaway car, whose driver, fearful of getting caught, left without waiting for everyone.

After the officers took the stocking off the black girl's face, they prepared her to be photographed. A deeply wrinkled officer held the girl's arms while the camera was loaded. Unlike the younger policemen, he seemed bored. Because the embarrassed girl kept staring at the floor, the officer pulled up her head by her bushy natural to expose her face. After taking her picture, the police led the girl to the paddy wagon parked outside on Nineteenth Avenue, where the male student guarded by two officers waited, his hands handcuffed behind him. A crowd of students gathered about the van, staring at the officers. Some of them commented on the contrast between the self-satisfied posture of the police and the handcuffed, helpless black student, with whom they readily identified. Other bystanders seemed to be rejoicing at the ritual of the arrest. One of them yelled approvingly, "Get the blackie!" A few turned to look at him pityingly and then looked back to watch the van take off.

At the noon rally that day, black students told the crowd that they should leave campus for the day. "That's what we're telling all black people, to split, and we're advising you to do the same." This advice sounded to many like warning of further violence, but the blacks had no more plans for disruption, nor were there any other incidents that day. Before leaving campus, white strike supporters held a meeting in the Gallery Lounge. To rouse the whites, Jack Alexis told them that from next week on they "would have to lead the struggle." He knew that the BSU's enthusiasm was already waning, but he believed that the white students might be able to reactivate the strike. "We're going to have a three-day weekend, and we should use that time to organize," he told the white students, who welcomed advice from a BSU spokesman at a time when the black students were still reluctant to deal with whites.

Organizing during that weekend consisted only of reminiscing about the events of the previous three days. On Tuesday, November 12, there were only a noon rally at the Speakers' Platform and minor incidents in front of the Psychology Building, until eight police officers assigned to the Psychology Building arrested twelve black students, who, rather than disrupting classes, had merely been walking down the halls. An excited white student who had witnessed their arrest ran immediately to the Speakers' Platform some fifty yards east of the Psychology Building and told the crowd that black students were being arrested without cause. Without a suggestion from the Speakers' Platform, the crowd began to march on the Psychology Building with cries of "Pigs!" There they stood and glared at the police while the arrested students were being photographed, urging by their shouts the alternatives of release of the blacks or an attack on the police. The police released the students, amid cheers and applause.

Later in the day, three white program students, inspired by the blacks, attempted to conduct their own "guerrilla" warfare. A corpulent white student who had brought two walkie-talkie sets to campus put himself in charge. He sent the first of his friends to survey the gym, where it was rumored that San Francisco police officers were stationed. As the spy went into the boiler room of the building, he found himself face-to-face with the police. Before he lost contact with his superior, he managed to report that the police were in the boiler room. The second student was sent to confirm this report. He too walked straight into the boiler room. The last time he was heard on the walkie-talkie, he was saying, "Man, they're here." Having received this report, his commander fled. He would say later with chuckles, his cheeks wobbling, "Man, I didn't want to get caught."

That night, when the Central Committee of the BSU met, their discussion centered around mobilization of the whites. The blacks knew that they could not continue the strike alone, and they wished the conflict over. The events of the last six days had exhausted all of them, although they would never have admitted it. They had not planned to strike any more than a day. Besides, many of them felt that they had already achieved more than they had expected. They scheduled a press conference for the following day, Wednesday, which would be their first since they had announced their intention to strike. The undisclosed purpose of the press conference was to prepare the public for the end of the strike. As Jack Alexis would say later, "It was implicitly understood by the leaders that the strike would die out by itself, and the press conference served to show that we would not give up our struggle even though the strike might die out from lack of support."

That day the mood on campus was uneasy. Some students went to classes. Others who supported the strike, numbering no more than 500, stayed away. They stood in front of the cafeteria, talking, reading the paper, enjoying the sun. Newsmen, by now familiar with the campus, could be seen walking about casually, not expecting anything noteworthy to occur that day. Word had it that the BSU had a press conference scheduled around noon, so the members of the press were enjoying themselves until then. As they began to gather in front of the BSU office after twelve, they attracted many curious students. The white students asked each other why the reporters were gathering. Some students who were not interested in the press conference went to stand before the Speakers' Platform to gossip about the events of the strike.

Shortly after twelve-thirty, the Central Committee members emerged from their office and went behind their barrackslike hut. The press followed. Leaning against the wall, the blacks huddled together, perhaps to be sure they were all on TV film. In their midst was George Murray, who read a prepared state· ment. Murray told the almost exclusively white press corps that the "disruptions" of the past six days had "historic signifi· cance" because for the first time in the United States people of color had fought side by side. When asked by the journalists what the black students' plans were, or if his statement meant the end of the strike, Murray replied: "You can tell every racist pig in the world, including Richard Milhouse Nixon, that we're not going to negotiate until our demands are met."

As the press conference broke up, about one o'clock, the newsmen dispersed. Those who were last to leave saw fourteen police officers going between the cafeteria and the huts. In pairs, the members of the Tactical Squad posted themselves be· fore the BSU office. Students who saw them followed and stood watching. Students coming out of classes joined these groups. In front of the BSU headquarters, black students glared at the police lines and, putting their heads together, began to talk. The sergeant was walking up and down the line, every now and then looking in the direction of the blacks. He talked to his men, who smiled and sometimes laughed faintly. Every one of the officers held his thirty-inch nightstick diago· nally across his chest. Except for the sergeant, who was tall and so thin that his cheekbones stood out, the officers, all over six feet tall, were heavyset.

As more students joined the group, the catcalls increased. Some students had speculated earlier that the officers were going to serve outstanding warrants on black student leaders. Others guessed that they had come to make arrests. Now, after seeing the policemen's smiling faces, the students decided that this was a show of force designed to counteract the BSU press conference.

"Pigs off campus" a few students yelled. Others joined in: "Pigs off campus." But still other students stood listening to these cries in disapproval.

Now some students began to hurl missiles over the heads of the Tactical Squad. Most threw clods of dirt, which they picked up from the ground, but some flung salt shakers stolen from the cafeteria, where salt and pepper shakers would soon be emptied and removed and their contents placed on the tables in open plastic cups to avoid such thefts. The police merely smiled, making efforts to avoid the missiles. Occasionally, one of the objects hit a helmet, raising howls and cheers.

Pushing the antenna of his walkie-talkie in and putting the instrument into its leather case, which dangled from his belt, the sergeant signaled his men to move. This made the students decide that the police were retreating, so they began to clap and to intensify their shouts. After the police had advanced some five yards, the sergeant angrily ordered his men to "get them." Now the officers began to run, hesitating only momentarily before clubbing the students, who were caught by surprise. Not expecting such an attack, they had been following the police closely. The police began to push the students on their way, clubbing those who didn't move fast enough. Girls screamed. Once at a safe distance, the students stopped to swear at the officers. One student fell over the steps leading to one of the huts which line the narrow path and lay bleeding. Two officers, having given the fallen student a few blows, now rushed toward others who had stopped to look back. Now the students pushed and trampled over each other, sprinting through the narrow passages between the huts. Two of the policemen chose to run up the path to the Bookstore, swinging their Japanese-made nightsticks. Six others headed toward the BSU office, where the black students stood aghast. As the police approached, the blacks began to run in different directions, some of them taking refuge in the office. Others hastily jumped over the square-trimmed hedge which separates the path between the Redwood Room and the BSU office. A larger number took an easier way, running behind the hut.

Nesbitt Crutchfield joined the latter group, picking up a three-foot stick from the ground as he fled. The officers caught up with him halfway between the huts. One of them swung his nightstick down on the black student's head. Suddenly Crutchfield was surrounded, the stick still in his hand. Two officers remained to guard him. The others ran on, continuing to pursue the blacks. Pushing Crutchfield against a wall, the two policemen grabbed their clubs with both hands and thrust them repeatedly into his stomach. Crutchfield doubled over. In the sunlight, his forehead shone with sweat. Then the officers began to punch him in the back, to knock him down. By now, Crutchfield was lying on the ground, covering his head with his hands, his legs folded up. One of the officers continually pushed his knee into the student's back, while the other thrust away with his club. As soon as Crutchfield stopped trying to protect himself, the officers dragged him away to the nearest police van. He would be charged, among other offenses, with "intent to assault a police officer."

Policemen chasing the students who had run from the BSU office soon arrested another student, but—unlike those who had arrested Crutchfield—they found themselves threatened by angry students surrounding them. Two other officers began to make their way toward a van parked behind the Bookstore. As TV cameramen filmed the scene, they were pushed to the wall, surrounded by shouting students. One of them pulled out his gun desperately and, crouching, pointed it at the students who continued to shout. Now students coming out of the buildings ran toward the noise. When they approached the crowd and saw the officer pointing his gun at the students, one of them said, "You're very brave, aren't you? You must be proud of yourself." He followed at a safe distance, taunting the police as they moved on to the paddy wagon where officers were booking arrested students.

Another pair of officers had been engaged in a chase which had taken them all the way to the other side of the central campus lawn. After a brief scuffle, they arrested a tall black student wearing a T-shirt. As they took him behind the Bookstore, they were surrounded. One of the officers drew his gun and, twisting the black student's hands behind his back, pushed him toward the paddy wagon. Students continued to follow. Every few yards the officer holding the gun would turn around and dare the students to come on. Once the group had crossed the lawn, five black students came out behind the bushes. When they saw one of their number, his arm twisted behind his back, his shirt pushed up, exposing his midriff, and an expression of pain on his face, they stopped.

Jack Alexis was one of this group. Grinding his teeth and clenching his fists, he mumbled to his friends as the officer went by a few yards away. Then, cursing, he struck out at white students who were standing nearby. Before he succeeded in hitting them, one of his black companions grabbed Alexis around the waist and the others pinned his arms down. "Let me go!" Alexis shouted in anguish. "They're taking my people away." Suddenly he managed to get loose and went after the police. But once again his companions pulled him back. "I don't care," he moaned. "Let me go. Let me go!" Alexis' friends led him away toward the huts.

Aware that their presence made the police uneasy, students continued to follow them. Behind the Bookstore, they stood by until the police boarded their paddy wagon. Then they followed behind and, after the wagons pulled out onto the street, stood watching them drive off.

A few students began to whisper to each other, pointing at the cameraman of a local television station, who was heading toward his station wagon parked nearby. Only a few minutes earlier, the cameraman had hit a student over the head with his camera and knocked him bleeding to the ground. The man hastened his pace, but the students followed persistently. Then one of the police vans, which was driving idly west on Holloway Avenue, stopped and two policemen emerged from the back door. Without hesitating, they ran toward the crowd and grabbed two of the students who were closest to the cameraman, hitting them with their nightsticks. As one of the students fell, the policemen continued to hit him, mumbling angrily. His mate hit away at the other student less passionately, every now and then stopping to jab him in the ribs. When students standing by increased their cries of "Pigs," other officers rushed out of the paddy wagons to form a protective circle around the two, who by now were dragging the beaten students by the hands to the paddy wagon. As soon as they had boarded, the other officers joined them and they sped away. The students, weary and unsure of what to do next, drifted back to the central campus area and the Speakers' Platform to see what would happen next.

As students came out of their classes, the crowd grew larger, and one student recognized a plainclothes officer who was wearing a black leather jacket and dark glasses, apparently in an effort to pass for a student. Incredulously, he pointed out the "pig" to those standing around him, and soon everyone was chanting "Pigs off campus" again. When the frightened plainclothesman quickly attempted to leave the crowd, the students followed. As he ran toward the Psychology Building to take refuge there among other officers, he was followed inside. Hearing shouts, a new crowd gathered. When the plainclothesman did not find any officers inside, he ran out of the building again, and entered the Education Building across the path. The students ran after him, but this time they were met by two uniformed officers stationed inside. By now, some two thousand students were shouting "Pigs off campus," and it looked as if they were warming up for an attack. The officers immediately summoned help and were soon joined by a dozen others who had also been inside the building. Moving out, they began to make their way off campus, frequently stopping and turning on the crowd, while the students showered them with missiles, including an occasional lead pipe or rock. Then, unexpectedly, some forty faculty pickets coming from the direction of the Gallery Lounge walked between the students and the police. After the faculty members had reassured the policeman that the students would stop following them, the officers left the campus and the crowd returned to the Speakers' Platform, where professors and students analyzed the day's events.

In a shaking voice, Jack Alexis told the angry crowd that there was much to be done. "We have to shut down the other state colleges until all our demands are met," he said. Alexis now felt that his rejected plans for the following semester could be put into practice. It seemed to him that Carmichael's prediction was becoming a reality, that the example of San Francisco State would be duplicated overnight. Now the crowd agreed to march on the Administration Building and meet with Smith, who was already conferring with his staff about what to do next. When he met with black students after the rally, Alexis and the others continually asked the president why he had called the police.

That day, Robert Smith had gone off campus for lunch with some of his aides, the events of previous days and the reports he had been given leading him to anticipate that the campus would be peaceful during his absence. Around noon, when one of his aides who was left on campus had been told that a campus policeman had been severely beaten by black students and that a TV cameraman had been jumped, he took on the responsibility of asking the police to intervene. Smith himself had always been careful to summon the police only to prevent violence or vandalism, and he always attempted to restrict them to a particular area. Upon his return from lunch, he found the college in chaos. That day his staff agreed, except for the aide who had made the decision, that letting the police loose on campus had been a mistake.

7

Solidarity Forever

O N FRIDAY AFTERNOON, NOVEMBER 1, WHEN PRESIDENT
Robert Smith announced that he was complying with the
chancellor's order to suspend black instructor George
Murray, a group of philosophy students and teachers were listening to a guest speaker in one of the classrooms in the HLL
Building. That evening, five professors who had listened to the
speaker left the campus and went to a small tavern nearby
where they discussed the lecture. This was to be the last time
they would discuss philosophy in 1968. Around eleven o'clock,
as the saloon keeper reminded them for the last time that he
was closing, they touched on the Murray case for a few minutes.
After gulping the remainder of their beer, they parted company
for that weekend, having decided that they should do something
about the suspension of George Murray.

Peter Radcliffe was one of the professors at the bar. He had
been teaching at the college for six years, and like his companions, had been an active member of the American Federation
of Teachers during that time. That semester, he had been
elected to the Executive Council of the Federation. Radcliffe
believed that the organization should intervene on Murray's

behalf because the black instructor was a member of the Union
—although not an active one—and because his public statements, no matter how outrageous, were not grounds for dis-
missal.

On Monday afternoon, the sandy-haired, bushy-bearded
Radcliffe met with the other members of the Executive
Council. The group passed a resolution which read:

> Recognizing the validity of many grievances of the Black
> Student Union, and recognizing the extreme violation of all
> due process and right governance of an academic community,
> as indicated by Chancellor Dumke's dictatorial action with
> regard to George Murray, we therefore support the strike
> presently called for, we urge individual union members to
> act in support of the proposed strike, and we call for the
> resignation of Chancellor Dumke, who has proven himself
> no longer a reputable member of the academic community.

This resolution surprised many professors and students, who
found it very militant, even for the liberal AFT.

The union at San Francisco State had been founded in 1960
by two professors, Arthur Bierman of the Philosophy Department and Herbert Williams of Anthropology. Like many professors in the union, Bierman is civic-minded. He thinks of his
college as one of the nation's best urban institutions. As such,
he believes, San Francisco State should respond to the needs of
the community in which it is located. Gentle, friendly, Bierman can often be seen talking with his students, his whole
body in motion and on his face a smile so large that he appears
to be laughing. One might easily think he is joking when he is
not. Yet his casual remarks have the organization of lectures,
and frequently, as he makes a point, he smiles and asks, "You
see?"

Bierman founded the AFT with Williams the year after the
House Un-American Activities Committee held its first hearings in San Francisco in 1959. The Committee offended many
in the Bay Area, especially after teachers the Committee had

called were fired. Although he was not directly involved in the hearings, Bierman joined the protestors, but he soon came to feel that demonstrations were not enough. It seemed to him that a good deal of energy was going to waste. When the Committee returned to San Francisco the following year, he organized SAFE, San Franciscans for Freedom in Education. Through careful planning, he obtained the support of San Francisco's Episcopal Bishop, and had the executive secretary of the labor council draw up a resolution demanding that HUAC stay out of California. HUAC called off its hearings and left the city. Bierman says, "This was a significant victory. It was banner news all across the nation. It was the beginning of a decline. You see?" He recalls cheerfully, "They made a movie about it, 'Operation Abolition,' which they are still showing."

Around this time, Bierman came to believe that teachers' vulnerability to political attack was due to their lack of organization. One day in the summer of 1960, while he was doing house painting "to make some money," Bierman began to think about getting his colleagues at San Francisco State to form a union. He and his friend Herbert Williams had already discussed this subject, but they had never tried to organize. Setting paint and brush aside, Bierman went straight to Williams' home, where over beer they mapped out a plan. The two phoned colleagues whom they thought would respond favorably. In about an hour they had thirty pledges and plenty of encouragement.

That fall, the American Federation of Teachers was officially established at San Francisco State, and through the next eight years it would bear Bierman's mark. He served as its president, sat on its Executive Council, and, when he didn't hold office, retained a power base in the organization and influenced its decision-making.

Socially liberal, he has made his home since 1952 in the Haight-Ashbury district, a section of San Francisco which, before the rise and fall of the Hippie Movement, was the pride of the natives. There, professors—many of them union members or sympathizers—students, workers, black and white, lived peacefully side by side. Bierman's appearance suggests the old district. He seldom wears a suit, and his fine, loose hair, which is combed straight back, makes him look like an English immigration officer. His baggy jacket is worn over a sweater. Bierman has exaggerated the English quality of his looks in a picture that hangs in the headquarters of the American Federation of Teachers. In it, he is wearing a bowler hat, and he has an umbrella hanging from his wrist. He is reading a newspaper, and smoking a long, fat cigar. Bierman says, "Habit, conformity, convention bother me more than anything else."

This attitude made Bierman accept the black students' attempts to by-pass conventional processes. His own experiences also made him sympathetic to them. After World War II, in 1946, he hitchhiked from Nebraska to Michigan to do graduate work at the university. Knowing that the deadline for applications had passed and that he would not be accepted, Bierman went directly to the dean, who admitted him. "He was really impressed. It was the conventional American story of making an effort," Bierman recounts.

Bierman felt that the conflict between the administration and students should never have been allowed to develop so far that on November 6 police were called to the campus which later that day had to be closed. Still hoping that once the national elections were over, sanity would prevail and that normality would be restored at San Francisco State, he left San Francisco the next day to go to Tampa, where he was going to deliver a series of lectures on "Philosophy of Urban Existence" at the University of Southern Florida.

That morning in San Francisco, economics professor William Stanton arrived on campus, still disgusted at the firing of George Murray several days before, and expecting the worst. Honoring the student strike, he had canceled his classes for the day. When he dropped into the office of the department to pick up his mail, he met other professors and discussed the situation at the college. On the basis of his experience as a former assemblyman and as a lawyer, Stanton urged his colleagues to vote as a department in favor of Murray's reinstatement. He cited examples of violent incidents on campus the previous day. In the modest Ecomonics Laboratory, sometimes referred to as the Econ Lounge, Stanton introduced and successfully obtained his colleagues' unanimous support of a motion later to be introduced, debated, amended, tabled, and reintroduced at various faculty meetings. It recommended that the entire faculty go on strike and ask for the resignation of Chancellor Glen Dumke.

News of the Econ Department's vote reached other departments in a matter of minutes. The first to follow suit was Philosophy. Most of the faculty in this department belonged to Local 1352, but were hesitant to involve their department in controversy over the strike. But once a "recommendation" from the economists arrived, the members felt free to call their own meeting to discuss the issues. Early on the morning of the following day, members of the philosophy faculty met and voted unanimously to voice their concern about the manner of George Murray's suspension. They did not go as far as Stanton and his colleagues had in recommending that the faculty strike.

After the meeting broke up, members of the Department of Philosophy went to the Economics Department, to meet other professors from different departments in the School of Humanities. These professors had been unable either to get their fellow department members to act in concert, or to find time to organize meetings. As if instinctively, they sought out those who had been able to take a strong stand.

The long, narrow, windowless hallway was soon crowded with those who had come to find an answer to the many problems which had arisen for them in the past six days since the suspension of the Black Panther teaching assistant. Many of them thought the campus violence of the previous two days was caused by the firing of the young black. Those who knew that a student strike had been planned long before President Robert Smith had suspended Murray conjectured that, without that suspension, events would not have been as violent. Whatever their individual analyses, they were all impressed with the decision of William Stanton and the other professors in economics. Peter Radcliffe recalls that the members of the Philosophy Department went through a dramatic change that morning. People who had not dared to think of the possibility of a teachers' strike to try to settle the crisis began to understand the radical and militant point of view. Everyone expressed resentment and anxiety at the chancellor's ignoring due process in the case of George Murray, and although no one was emotionally prepared to threaten a strike himself, each felt drawn to someone who had. Of the hundred or so professors in the Econ Lounge on Friday, November 8, sixty-seven voted to send an ultimatum to President Smith, pledging to go on strike if he did not respond favorably. Stanton was their natural choice for emissary, for he was the most militant and politically experienced.

In the early sixties, when he was teaching at San Jose State College, an urban institution like San Francisco State, Stanton had battled against the administration and the trustees over the firing of a black instructor. This resulted in the loss of his teaching position. Though the decision was appealed, the U.S. Supreme Court upheld the administration's decision. Leaving the academic world, Stanton carried his fight for justice to the State Assembly for two two-year terms. Bored and disappointed with his less-educated peers in the Assembly and rejected by his constituency, Stanton went back to teaching in 1967, this time at San Francisco State. For him there was no memory of the "good old days" at State, no relaxed intellectual atmosphere to look back on with nostalgia. To Stanton, the firing of Murray was an "outright act of racism," and he told his colleagues that day that a strike threat was their only alternative.

Stanton was to lead a delegation from the group, by now ti-
tled the Ad Hoc Faculty Committee, to express its concern
and present its ultimatum. Around 11:30, while the white radical students were preparing for their noon rally and the black
students were carrying on guerrilla raids on various department
offices, President Smith's secretary informed him that there was
a delegation of faculty members in the outer office waiting to
see him. Having been at the institution for the last twenty
years and still attempting to be as informal as possible, Smith
stepped out to greet them personally. After a warm welcome,
he took the professors into then-Vice-President Devere Pentony's office, where he was discussing the crisis on campus with
other administrators. "Well, what can I do for you?" he began.

Behind the thick lenses of Stanton's glasses, his myopic eyes
looked even smaller than their actual size, as he told Robert
Smith that the chancellor's order was racist. He said that it was
also a threat to the entire faculty because if one teacher could
be suspended artibrarily, it could happen to others. "We have
decided that if Murray is not reinstated by next Tuesday at five
o'clock, we'll go on strike the next day," Stanton said. He
added, in tones which seemed to betray fatigue: "You
shouldn't view this as a personal attack. We're not your
enemies." Unlike the other professors in the delegation, Stanton preferred to argue from a practical viewpoint. And to him,
the practical thing seemed to be for Smith to be sensible, grant
the kids' demands, and get this over with. Stanton sounded
tired, almost as if he would give up the fight any day now. But
during the four and one half months when police were on campus every school day, he always showed up. One day,
while being questioned by a television reporter, Stanton turned
to the camera—his audience—and said, in a desperate voice:
"Don't you see that we're here today for you, that what we are
doing is for your benefit?"

Smith, in turn, expressed to Stanton's delegation his own

dissatisfaction with the chancellor's decision, promising to do his best and adding that he didn't want to see them go out on strike. Stanton had told him that the group would be supported by at least another twenty-five professors on Wednesday morning, the deadline for Smith to reinstate Murray, if they were forced to go on strike. The Ad Hoc Committee delegation had come in smiling; they left the half-hour meeting with tempers still cool, for they were convinced that Smith was doing his best. As they stepped outside Pentony's office, some twenty Bay Area reporters and cameramen rushed to the delegation hoping for a new angle.

Hank McGucken, Professor of Speech, spoke for the group, telling the press of their ultimatum. He was assaulted with questions about how the proposed faculty strike was related to the student strike.

"Do you support the student strike?" asked a local TV reporter, in formal professional tones.

Blushing, visibly embarrassed at having to speak formally, McGucken said: "We are not officially connected with the student strike. We are only protesting the chancellor's order. As the kids say, 'We're doing our thing.' "

Unlike Stanton, McGucken had been at San Francisco State for some time. In 1955, he had enrolled as a student at the age of twenty-five, after serving two years in the Army in France. In five years at the college, he earned his B.A. and M.A. in English. During this time, he had met most of the faculty members in the School of Humanities which he would one day run as associate dean. His first teaching job was as a teaching assistant to the then-Professor of General Semantics S. I. Hayakawa. After two years at Stanford, where he took his Ph.D., McGucken was offered the position of assistant professor. Since 1961, he has been at State, which he finds "an exciting place" where young professors experiment freely with innovative teaching techniques, and where he can concentrate on teaching instead of on research. To McGucken, the recent interference by the chancellor of the state college system in the internal affairs of San Francisco State constituted a serious threat to the college. Earlier during the week of November 5, McGucken had resigned from the Academic Senate to protest George Murray's suspension.

The reporter continued his questioning with the hope of having McGucken admit that his group sympathized with the students' strike and perhaps with their tactics. "Professor McGucken, what do you think of the student disruptions?" he asked.

"The Ad Hoc Faculty Group is only affirming a principle, not supporting other people's methods," McGucken said to the group of journalists, now surrounded by student bystanders. "We have a long history of grievance at the chancellor's interfering in the affairs of this campus, and we have had enough. Our protest is against the chancellor, not the president. This is the last straw. The chancellor's action was precipitous and illogical. He acted against the advice of the president, the faculty, and the mayor of San Francisco."

That night McGucken appeared on the television screens of Bay Area homes. His remarks about his group doing its own thing sounded to many like an effort to appease the students while completely freeing "the kids" from responsibility in the upheaval. For the administration, faculty intervention formed the foundation of a crisis which was to last nearly five months. Without faculty support, the student strike would soon have ended. Later that semester, Vice-President of Academic Affairs Donald Garrity attributed the disruption at San Francisco State to members of the faculty like McGucken and Stanton. "If the teachers hadn't intervened, we would have solved the problem long ago," Donald Garrity said.

A handful of professors at San Francisco State that fall had already made up their minds about the issue of outside intervention in the college long before the crisis arose. Twenty-nine-year-old Anatol Anton, in philosophy, was expecting something to happen at State long before Murray was suspended. Anton expected a repeat of the early fifties, and he was determined to avoid the kind of mistakes his elder colleagues had made during the McCarthy Era. He felt that they had either not fought hard enough or had not fought at all. Now the pre-election day speeches by conservative politicians about "coming down hard" on blacks and white militant students seemed to him an indication of what would follow. Having ceased to be a student at Stanford only the previous year, Anton still identified with students and maintained close contacts with them.

Students often went to Anton to talk politics. Once he vowed in frustration, "I'm not going to talk to these students any more because they pick my brain for their articles and leaflets. As a matter of fact, two of them even wrote a book. I'm going to write my own stuff from now on instead of giving my ideas to others."

His informal garb and manners make it difficult to recognize Anton as a professor. He frequently wore a pair of khaki pants which fell below his waist, so that he had to keep pulling them up, and a wrinkled white dress shirt with no tie. Perhaps his unshaven face and tousled hair contributed most to his student appearance. Many students assumed Anton was one of them.

On Sunday, November 10, two days after the Stanton-McGucken delegation to Smith, Anton attended a white student strike support meeting at 55 Colton Street, the New Left headquarters in downtown San Francisco. He had originally planned to go directly to a faculty meeting in the home of English professor Mark Linenthal, but at the last minute decided to drop by Colton Street to find out what the students were doing. There he discovered that he had fallen behind on student thinking, when one of his ideas was turned down. He had suggested that big name entertainers and speakers be invited to campus to lure uncommitted students out of their classes. With ambiguous feelings about his involvement in student affairs, Anton left for the faculty meeting where he tried to convey to the professors the impatience which had been evident at the students' meeting he had just left. Although Anton decided that day that he should not interfere in student decisions, he continued to see his student friends. For him, the faculty's involvement in the crisis at San Francisco State was always part of the student strike.

The Sunday meeting at Linenthal's strengthened the Ad Hoc Faculty Group, which was beginning to acquire form and organization. After the Veterans' Day holiday, the militant professors returned to school on Tuesday, the deadline they had given Smith for reinstating Murray. They knew that they would have to strike. Without success, they attempted to get the entire faculty to vote for the strike. They did manage to have the entire body, which met in the Main Auditorium, pass a resolution asking for the resignation of Chancellor Dumke. This general faculty meeting, which the Ad Hoc Group had requested the previous week, did little to resolve the campus crisis. Instead, it offered a forum for professors to sound off on long-standing feuds with one other. The conservatives, or those who opposed the strike, were accused of hiding their incompetence as teachers behind the cloak of professionalism; the radicals, or those who sided with the students, were denounced as wanting a strike for its own sake. Someone even said that Stanton had wanted to go on strike since the day he began to teach at State. Amidst the arguments, Smith got up and told the faculty, "We're not out of the woods yet," and the chairman of the meeting unsuccessfully asked the body to give the president a vote of confidence. While the faculty was meeting in the Main Auditorium, students outside in the mid-campus area were holding a rally to denounce a professor who had proposed mediation between the strikers and the administration. Black Student Union Chairman Benny Stewart told the crowd, assembled under a warm, sunny sky: "Our demands are simple. We don't need any more proposals. Mediation would be just administrators talking to other administrators."

As was expected, the Ad Hoc Group's ultimatum to Smith went unanswered, and the militant faculty, true to their word, on Wednesday, November 13, formed the first faculty picket line in the history of San Francisco State at the main entrance to the campus, the corner of Nineteenth and Holloway Avenues. The decision to strike had come the previous night, when the group had met for several hours at one of the professor's homes. McGucken and others who had accompanied him to deliver the ultimatum to President Smith insisted that they had made a public commitment on which they should follow through. As they began to discuss picket signs, they realized that they were actually going to strike. Ted Keller remembered that he had some $8\frac{1}{2}''$ x $11''$ red paper, and a friend who would print the signs free of charge. At 7:30 the following morning, the first faculty pickets appeared, demanding autonomy and due process.

McGucken now says that though "that was a mini-strike, it infuriated many professors. They thought we wouldn't dare." Peter Radcliffe remembers that, for many, the strike was "a test of manhood." In the past, the faculty had always been ignored by the trustees of the college system. The Ad Hoc group of professors saw the faculty as powerless, the final say about everything belonging to the trustees. The trustees, who come from the business circles of the state of California, have often looked upon the teachers, particularly those from the School of Humanities, as impractical, imcompetent intellectuals.

On Wednesday morning, November 13, as the time for the second day of the faculty meeting drew near, the pickets gradually retreated to the Main Auditorium to attend one of the long and continuous assemblies which were to take place throughout the period Smith was president. As the morning session came to an end, the faculty broke up into various cliques for lunch and strategy meetings. Stanton, thinking that all their efforts were futile, went instead to the Speakers' Platform to listen to the students. "It's just a big farce," he told a student who asked him what was going on at the faculty meeting. "Those guys don't know what they're talking about." But he decided nevertheless to return to the meeting, saying, "I'd better go and see what they'll do now."

Near the entrance to the Creative Arts Building, which houses the Main Auditorium, Stanton met other members of the Ad Hoc Group. By now, his had become a familiar face to everyone on campus. He had appeared on TV and had been quoted by the local newspapers. Students slowed down to catch a glimpse of the "wild-eyed radical professor," and whispered to their companions, "That's Stanton." Stanton himself pointed out to his companions professors who had condemned the students during the meeting of the previous day, and occasionally raised his voice in terming them "reactionary" or "bigot."

After some small talk, he was turning down the hall toward the direction of the auditorium when he saw a student run by. Noticing Stanton, he stopped. Trying to catch his breath, he reported, "The pigs are beating up students." "Where?" Stanton asked. "Down by the Gallery Lounge," the student yelled, hoping apparently to get some sympathetic faculty members to intervene.

Almost running himself, Stanton went outside the building where he saw students hurrying toward the Gallery Lounge. He followed. As he approached the path between the lounge and the Education Building, he saw a large group of screaming students. Coming closer, he heard applause, and saw the line of some forty faculty members who had just separated the blue uniformed police officers from the students taunting them.

Earlier in the afternoon, behind the hut which houses its office, the BSU had given its first press conference since the strike began. Shortly afterward, the tall, thin sergeant had placed fourteen members of the Tactical Squad in front of the office and eventually had ordered them to charge on the students who were taunting them. The officers had indiscriminately hit everyone in sight and singled out blacks for arrest.

Elsewhere on campus, students had gathered, their tempers hot, around twenty or so additional policemen who had apparently been attempting to leave the area. As the chants of "Pigs off campus" grew louder, many other students joined the crowd. When the police were in the passageway near the Gallery Lounge and between the Psychology and Education Buildings, the students began to throw objects like lead pipes and dirt. Although none of the missiles hit the policemen, the angry sergeant ordered his men to charge. Making a quick 180-degree turn, they ran after the students, who immediately retreated.

Realizing that he had acted hastily, the sergeant called his men back and instructed them to form two lines, one facing the students to protect another that was withdrawing five yards behind. The withdrawing line would then turn to face the students, while the other began to retreat behind its guard. This tactic was apparently used to discourage the students from attack. Those who were close to the police didn't throw anything, but those behind the first rows felt free to hurl anything they could find. Furious, the sergeant gave up his complicated tactic of withdrawal and ordered his men to march on the students. It was at this moment that the red picket signs appeared in single formation as the professors walked right between the students and the police.

To the student members of the Progressive Labor Party, this faculty march constituted interfering in the internal affairs of students, and a handful of members told the professors to "get the Hell out of here." Anton, who had been walking with his colleagues a few minutes earlier, was chastised by the son of a San Francisco contractor. A San Francisco State student who aspired to membership in PL, he was a member of the

Worker-Student Alliance of SDS. Most of the other students, though, greeted their professors with cheers and applause, kisses and hugs. A girl student threw her arms around Kay Boyle's neck, tears in her eyes, and kissed the novelist-professor on the cheeks. Another girl shook the professor's hands. Some students patted their teachers on the back as they passed by. Stanton had arrived as the teachers were drawing the line of demarcation, and he found himself between his colleagues and the police, who had their batons pointing at the professors and the students behind them. Quickly, because he had no picket sign to identify him as faculty member rather than student, Stanton joined his colleagues.

After a standstill of almost three minutes, the police resumed their retreat. But the Progressive Labor wing of the demonstrators started showering rocks on the officers, who turned around ready to charge. Before they could do so, Stanton withdrew from the lines, moved forward, and stopped a few yards from the officers. He turned toward the students and raised his hands. "Go back! Go back!" he pleaded. "They are leaving and that's what we want." Despite scattered complaints, he continued. "Let's go back to the Speakers' Platform. We're going to hold a rally."

PL members retorted, "Get out of here. That's none of your business. Why don't you mind your own affairs?" But the overwhelming number of students was too glad to see the police leave to reject Stanton's suggestion.

Stanton and the other professors who had "put their bodies on the line" felt only relief that another day had come to an end without loss of life. "Any fool should realize the danger to life caused on this campus by the action of suspending Murray," Stanton told reporters that afternoon. "I tell you, if it goes on like this somebody's going to get killed."

Five minutes later, the police had disappeared, and students and faculty members had assembled at the Speakers' Platform.

The rally being his suggestion, Stanton grabbed the microphone to tell the students angrily, "WE'RE GOING TO CLOSE THIS FUCKING CAMPUS DOWN!" His angry audience agreed.

That afternoon President Smith ordered the campus closed indefinitely until it should again become a safe place to work and study. He told a relieved faculty, "Bringing in police in an effort to keep this campus open has not worked to my satisfaction."

The next day, Thursday, November 14, in Tampa, Art Bierman, after lecturing at the university, returned to his friend's home to review the previous night's work he had done with his host and co-editor. In his room, he found a letter from his wife, giving a lengthy and detailed account of the incidents that had taken place at San Francisco State. She enclosed clippings from the Bay Area papers of Friday and Saturday which stated that over sixty professors, calling themselves the Ad Hoc Faculty Committee, were threatening to go on strike over Murray's suspension. In her letter, Mrs. Bierman, who is an experienced community worker, argued that settling the professors grievances by striking was a good idea, but that the group lacked organization. Susan Bierman had been active in her neighborhood, most recently in the battle against building a freeway through the city, and Bierman felt she was an astute political analyst. By the time he had finished reading the clippings, his friend James Gould had returned. "Things don't seem to be going very well in San Francisco," Bierman told his host worriedly.

Later that afternoon, when they watched the news on TV, Bierman saw the reports on San Francisco State and viewed his own colleagues marching on the path between the Education Building and the Gallery Lounge to form a single line between police and students. Later, William Stanton appeared on the screen, worried and emotional, cautioning the audience against hostility toward the students and telling them that they were being "had" by the politicians. Bierman, drawing on his cigar, felt certain that his wife was right. There had to be more organization, and an appeal on bread-and-butter issues should be worked up in order to get the public's support. Now the governor was on the screen, denouncing President Smith, calling the closing of San Francisco State an "unprecedented act of irresponsibility," and demanding that the college be reopened immediately.

Bierman spent the next four days as he finished his work in Tampa planning what he would do when he returned. The day he was boarding his plane to return to San Francisco, President Smith told a faculty meeting that he was going to reopen the campus the following day, Wednesday, November 20, because the trustees had ordered him to do so. After his announcement, amidst what many regarded as total confusion, Professor of Social Welfare Mario D'Angeli suggested that the faculty hold a convocation where both the administration and the student strike leaders could sit down and discuss the strike demands. Hesitantly, the faculty agreed. In planning to reopen the college, which had been closed for four school days, Smith was following a directive which in his judgment was faulty, just as he had, earlier, in suspending George Murray. The trustees had ordered Smith to open the campus and let classes be resumed on a normal basis. Smith knew well that this could not be accomplished, yet he attempted to carry out their order. The realities of life at San Francisco State required other action. When the faculty planned to conduct discussions about the causes of the strike instead of teaching, they were acting more out of anger at the trustees than in support of the students. Some people argued that the students would use these convocations to humiliate the administration publicly.

The same day, Bierman arrived at the San Francisco Airport at 7 P.M. and, after some difficulty starting the eleven-year-old battered Volvo which he had purchased the previous year, drove straight home. Without wasting time, he started to go over the clippings his wife had saved for him. By midnight, the dining room table was covered with these clippings and his notes. Bierman now felt that he had a clear understanding of the situation, and wanted to verify it with the impressions of his long-time friend and co-founder of Local 1352, Herbert Williams. When Bierman phoned him, Williams agreed. They had to organize and make the issues real to the public. There was definitely a need for a plan of action and for propaganda to explain the teachers' position.

Bierman says he then put in three twenty-hour days talking to various faculty members in order to explain what was needed. He gained new support the following week when the trustees dismissed the administration's efforts to settle the crisis through discussions and insisted that normal instruction be resumed at the college. These resentful professors felt that the trustees should not override the president, especially during a crisis.

Then Chairman of the Board of Trustees Theodore Meriam, general manager of a department store in central California, publicly derided the idea of a convocation. Insisting that the college be reopened, he said: "Quite obviously there is a portion of the faculty at State which has chosen to defy the people of the State of California. It is difficult to regard these people as professional members of the college faculty. I am confident that the Board of Trustees will not overlook the performance that has been going on at this particular college. Correctional steps are mandatory. Apparently these faculty activists have lost any sense of responsibility." Meriam concluded angrily, "The trustees at their next meeting will act in whatever manner is deemed necessary to end this disgraceful, unprofessional, and unrealistic situation."

Such statements continued to appear in the papers, to the dismay of many professors who felt that Meriam's remarks were directed against them. Worried about their future, they met that week at Temple Judea, about a mile south of campus, safe from police and students alike.

After allowing time for the expression of fears, Bierman

arose. Pushing his glasses up off his nose, he said: "Many people here are talking about a strike. A strike in order to be effective has to have the sanction of the Labor Council, and should be called by a union which is a member of the Labor Council." He was referring to an arrangement existing in the City of San Francisco whereby any striking union wanting the support of the other unions in the city had to have the sanction of the Labor Council. Bierman continued, "I know that there are many among you who are not members of the local. How many of you are not members?" he asked. The one-third of the audience who did not belong to the AFT then signed up. Bierman then explained the need for a program, a superb organization. Many in the audience who believed that their union could never get the Labor Council's sanction urged that they go on strike without being associated with organized labor, although the majority preferred the security of having a powerful group like the Labor Council behind them. Only a minority felt that it would soil the professors to be associated with AFL-CIO and the labor leaders who had publicly supported the war in Viet Nam.

Bierman thought that it was still too early to ask for the strike sanction. Time was needed to enlist more professors in the AFT and to make the crisis situation clearer to the public. On Monday, November 25, the convocation resumed, having been temporarily interrupted over the issue of whether or not all students should participate. After several hours of discussion between administrators, students, and members of the Academic Senate, it had been agreed that a three-day convocation would be held.

On the first day, the mood on campus was agitated. Students and professors could be seen going from one classroom to another until they found a room where the discussions were to their liking. In the Creative Arts Building, students were lounging against the walls exchanging the latest gossip. In the Education Building, where additional television sets had been

installed to monitor the main discussion, students and professors formed semicircles around each set so that they could listen attentively to the exchange. Every now and then, embarrassment became evident on the faces of these viewers when a
black student on the panel insulted an administrator.

During the opening of the convocation, Jerry Varnado, the
on-campus coordinator of the Black Student Union, had called
President Robert Smith a "pig." Later, when Smith asked Varnado how much time he needed to make his opening statement, the black student had replied contemptuously, "We're
going to take just as much time as we need."

Varnado was angry that morning. He felt that he had been
double-crossed by Nesbitt Crutchfield and Jack Alexis. During
the Central Committee meeting the night before, Varnado had
swayed the majority to his viewpoint that the black students
should boycott the convocation because open discussion would
weaken the BSU's position and overshadow their demands.
Crutchfield's and Alexis' joint resolution to continue the dia-
logue with the administration had been defeated. The following day, Varnado's position was presented to the general
membership for ratification. The BSU leaders were attempting
to secure maximum support from members and wished to come
before them as a united front. If necessary, each committee
member was to defend the majority position whether he agreed
with it or not. That day, Crutchfield arose at the general meeting and insisted that the committee's recommendation be discussed by the membership and put to a vote. During the discussion, he and Alexis argued against Varnado's view because
the convocation would be a means of recruiting more supporters within the college. As if this deviation from procedure were not enough, the two also proposed and obtained the
membership's approval to send Varnado as a delegate to the
convocation. Both Crutchfield and Alexis were subsequently
punished for insubordination. Punishment in such cases might
range from memorizing quotations from Mao's Red Book to

doing push-ups in the presence of the Central Committee members. In this case, both offenders were suspended from the Central Committee for two weeks. Crutchfield was ordered, in addition, to work on the Black Panther Breakfast Program during his suspension.

That day, the local educational television station, KQED, carried the meeting to the city. The convocation was recessed at 4:30 and Smith was summoned to Los Angeles to explain to the trustees how his actions complied with the specific orders he had received to resume normal teaching on campus.

On Tuesday, the following day, tension had risen. There was still distrust of the administration, this time about disciplinary letters sent to striking student leaders. That afternoon, as the main convocation was coming to an end, the Ad Hoc Faculty Committee gathered for its own meeting in the new wing of the HLL Building. Room 135, where they met, was typical of a trend that would take place in college buildings in the years to come as the number of students increased. Unlike the standard classrooms which could seat 35 to 40 students at most, 135 was built with tiers of seats so that it would accommodate more than one hundred students.

Shortly after four o'clock, a student came into the lecture room where all the seats were filled and many people were either standing along the walls or sitting on the steps. The student seemed to be searching for someone who wasn't in the auditorium. All of a sudden, noticing the bespectacled economics professor facing the audience, the student walked hurriedly to Stanton and, without saying a word, handed him a sheet of paper. Raising his eyebrows in disbelief, William Stanton read its contents a second time and burst out laughing. Quickly, the room was silenced as the crowd looked at him with apprehension. Pulling himself together, Stanton again looked over the contents of the sheet of paper, which had been copied from an Associated Press dispatch.

"Smith has resigned," he announced, "and they have appointed Hayakawa acting president."

"Hayakawa?" many questioned in unison.

"Hayakawa?" joined in others.

Those who had said "Hayakawa" first began to laugh first, as soon as they realized that it was indeed S. I. Hayakawa of San Francisco State who was to head the college. Hysterical laughter soon spread, many of the professors and students doubling over, their hands on their stomachs, like Stanton, in the laughter of shock.

Bierman, who was standing in the middle of the room facing the laughing group, only smiled. Then the smile left his face. Shaking his fist, he shouted repeatedly, "Strike! Strike! Strike!"

Within moments, laughter had given way to militant fist-shaking and angry shouts of "Strike! Strike!" The doubts of many of these men vanished in the short space of time it took Stanton to make them aware of the trustees' latest move. Now they knew that they had no choice but to strike.

8

The Bottom of the Barrel

WHILE THE LIBERAL FACULTY MEMBERS AND THEIR STUDENT allies were discussing the strike, a short, 150-pound man was in the Business Building nearby, talking to the chancellor on the telephone. S. I. Hayakawa was accepting the presidency of San Francisco State, which he had been offered only a few minutes earlier. The chancellor had accepted his one stipulation, reassuring him of the trustees' support, and the semantics professor, who had been at the college for thirteen years now, was about to begin a new period in his long and diversified career.

Earlier that day, Hayakawa had gone off campus to lunch with a group of conservative faculty members. After lunch, he returned to campus with Professor of Business Paul Juhls, who had managed a small real estate business on the West Coast before entering the academic world. When they arrived on campus shortly after three o'clock, Hayakawa seemed nervous and upset about the group's inability to end the crisis. Telling his companion that he wanted to call his private secretary to see if he had received any phone calls, Hayakawa asked Juhls for permission to use his phone in the BSS Building. When he spoke to his secretary, Hayakawa learned that the chancellor had called several times.

Earlier that day, President Robert Smith had been summoned to Los Angeles to attend an emergency meeting of the board of trustees. After spending most of the morning waiting in the hallway, Smith was finally called in and asked repeatedly if he would follow the trustees' directives about the campus crisis. The irritated Smith answered consistently that he would try to keep the college open, if it were safe for everyone on campus. He never told the trustees what they wanted to hear: that he would keep the campus open at any cost. Instead, as he had done earlier all during the crisis at San Francisco State, Smith tried that morning to get the trustees interested in the causes of the turmoil at the college. When the meeting broke up around noon, no agreement had been reached about how the crisis should be handled.

During lunch, at which Smith was the trustees' guest, he suddenly interrupted the informal conversation about events at State to say that he could solve their problem by resigning. He explained that he would request a transfer to his former position as professor of education. The trustees expressed shock, but their comments soon indicated that they accepted his decision. Some of them requested that he make a "low-key" statement to the press. Smith agreed to do so, although he would say afterward that he had extremely "high-key feelings" about his decision. Other trustees asked if he had any recommendation for a successor. Remembering that his previous suggestions to them had been ignored, Smith gave a negative reply, in a rather sarcastic tone. One of the trustees even asked if they could be of any help to Smith professionally. Only one man at the table objected to Smith's decision: Glen Dumke told the president that resigning was "poor professional ethics."

Smith ignored Dumke's remarks that day, but he might have reacted differently had he known what he would find out later from acquaintances at the college, that Dumke had already made plans to get rid of him. Dumke apparently felt rather awkward. He was supposed to make the trustees' job as smooth as possible, and he had obviously failed by recommending Smith as president. Now Dumke suggested Hayakawa. After being told what the semanticist's opinion on the turmoil at the college was, the trustees accepted the recommendation. Hayakawa would say later, "I guess they had reached the bottom of the barrel." After the trustees had decided on Hayakawa, Dumke went to work immediately. When he couldn't reach the semanticist either at his office or at home, he had left messages with Hayakawa's secretary and also with administrators.

Now Hayakawa stood replacing the receiver on Juhls' telephone, somewhat taken aback at the fact that he was to be acting president of the college. The one stipulation he had made before accepting was that he be free to call in police. The group had already made their policy clear on this, so Dumke was surprised to hear what Hayakawa wanted. The new acting president said later, "He thought I was laying down conditions about money or tenure or something like that."

"Well, congratulations," Juhls said, upon hearing the news. At Hayakawa's request, he had left the room while his colleague talked to the chancellor.

"I may even need your prayers," Hayakawa replied in the soft and humble voice he uses when he feels he is in friendly company. Then he went to his own office to call his wife and friends.

Shortly after he reached his office, there was a knock on the door. The college's public relations man had come to congratulate the new president and receive his orders. Harvey Yorke, a retired Air Force colonel, had been at the college almost a year. In Korea, and later in France under General Norstad, the former NATO commander, he had performed the same services as he did now at San Francisco State. Yorke proved to be the only college administrator who came to greet the new president. The two became a team which was to function smoothly throughout the entire crisis at the college and also during Hayakawa's short-lived and unannounced plans to run for political office. Now as the two walked toward the Administration Building, Yorke explained what their next move should be: first, a public statement.

A small crowd had already gathered to hear the new president's policies. Eric Solomon of the English Department was among them, muttering in anger as he paced up and down the hall, his ears bright red. Solomon was furious at the trustees' appointment and at Hayakawa's accepting it, but whenever anyone in the crowd asked the reason for his anger, he only uttered something incomprehensible. Like Solomon, Hayakawa was a member of the Presidential Selection Committee, a group of five professors chosen to screen prospective candidates for the presidency in order to make recommendations to the chancellor, who in turn would make a proposal to the trustees. The committee had agreed that any one of them who wished to become a candidate should first resign from the committee and notify its members of his decision. Hayakawa had simply ignored this agreement. The committee felt that in so doing, he had set a precedent for the trustees to bypass the faculty— who believed that the existence of the committee was a first step toward self-government for the college.

Later that afternoon, when Hayakawa was going to his first press conference, Solomon angrily asked, "Why did you accept the appointment? I thought we had an agreement."

"It was an emergency," Hayakawa replied, leading the group of reporters to the conference room.

Hayakawa's appointment was bleakly humorous to many professors and students at San Francisco State. It seemed to them that during a faculty meeting over a week earlier he had exhibited a complete lack of understanding about the crisis at the college. The professor of general semantics, who taught only one evening class, had accused the liberal faculty members of exaggerating the situation, of being the victim of their literary imaginations. "If we call our college racist, what term do we have left for the government of Rhodesia?" he had asked. His opponents had laughingly retorted, "Racist, Hayakawa, racist."

Those who remembered the Free Speech Movement of 1964 at the University of California in nearby Berkeley had an additional reason to be alarmed at Hayakawa's appointment. He had condemned the rebels at the university in the pages of the student daily at San Francisco State, while most of his colleagues were proudly pointing out that the FSM left their campus untouched because free speech was not threatened there.

Those who had been at the college longer laughed at his appointment for additional reasons, which dated back to shortly after his arrival on campus in 1955. He had come from Illinois Institute of Technology, at a time when well-known authors were being hired in the English Department at San Francisco State to build up its prestige. Soon after he began to teach at the college, some members of the department began to feel that Hayakawa was making it apparent to them that they were not as well-known as he and that their books had not sold as well as his *Language in Thought and Action*. His self-important attempts at leadership in the department were halted during a party at his home after he told his departmental colleagues that they should be teaching general semantics rather than English, proposing that the entire liberal arts college be replaced by a general semantics workshop in the woods, presumably under his direction. Many of those who heard him did not take him seriously. He often spoke out impulsively, sometimes intending to be witty. But others grew angry. As Hayakawa was enumerating the advantages of specializing in general semantics, author Mark Harris cut him short with the criticism that he was reducing their discipline to a business enterprise. The story has it that Hayakawa, refusing to talk to his guests, retired to a corner, took out the harmonica he always carries in his vest pocket, and began to play. From then on,

Hayakawa would be excluded from close intellectual groups in the department, and the tradition of looking down on him would grow. He would often be dismissed as a glib business-man in contrast to scholars who stood above material interests. Although this treatment hurt Hayakawa, it did not prevent him from considering himself an "internationally famous" se-manticist.

His behavior is never what one might expect from a college president. During a speech at the University of Colorado, while he was being booed by a hostile audience, he began to dance in time to the monotonous chant of the militant students. On his way to board a plane for Washington, where he was to testify before a Senate hearing on student unrest, he told reporters that one thing he liked about being acting president was that he didn't have to worry about getting fired, because it was only a temporary job.

Samuel Ichiye Hayakawa was born in Vancouver, British Co-lumbia, on July 18, 1906, the first son of an enterprising immi-grant from Japan, who had come to San Francisco at the turn of the century. After a brief stay, the young man returned to Japan to marry, and then chose Canada as his home. He named his first child after Samuel Johnson. The family moved frequently, as the father's business dealings took them to dif-ferent parts of Canada. His efforts were often lucrative, but he faced failure, too. One year when he was in the labor contract-ing business, an early frost destroyed the sugar beet crop and the Japanese laborers he had brought over to harvest it found themselves without work. Typically, S. I. Hayakawa stresses the bright side of this story. "My father at the age of eighty-six," he says, "now in Japan, is still very proud of the fact that these la-borers were wiped out so far as making a living was concerned, but that they pulled themselves together and some of them are still there. Their children and grandchildren are leading citi-zens of Southern Alberta to this day. They all stayed and worked hard, and prospered."

The boy began his schooling in Cranbrook, British Columbia, but by the time he had reached the eighth grade, had attended seven different schools. "Going to a new school every fall was standard operating procedure," he recalls. He went to high school in "the least fashionable part of Winnipeg, an area heavily populated by Russian Jews," he explains. "Two-thirds of the student body was Jewish, one-third English or Scotch, with a few Czechoslovaks and Poles." Hayakawa was the only Japanese in the school. Once again, he takes an optimistic view. "I was terribly good friends with everybody, including the Jewish kids," he says, and then adds, "and including the non-Jewish kids."

By the time Hayakawa had graduated from high school, his father was in the import-export business and wished his son to join him. But Hayakawa decided to go to the University of Manitoba instead. "It's the kind of streetcar college that you go to when you don't have any money to go to another school," he says. These were quiet years. He remembers that he "never went out for athletics, except to become the mascot of the hockey team," and says laughingly that he was "too damn small to play"—he pauses—"big kids." "—Big kids," he repeats. Size did not prevent him from participating in sports, though. He played some baseball, some lacrosse, some ice hockey, "but I never was big or strong enough to do anything important enough in any . . . " He leaves the sentence unfinished. During these years at Manitoba, Hayakawa joined the First Squadron, Canadian Machine Gun Corps, "a militia unit not connected with the college." He doesn't remember why he joined, because he has "never thought about it." Musing, he recalls, "I had some friends there. The commanding officer was my high school teacher. I admired him very much. That wasn't the reason I went, but I was glad he *was*." Hayakawa stayed in the unit long enough to be commissioned Canadian Army Scholar Lieutenant.

By 1927, he had graduated and moved to Montreal, where he

received his M.A. in English. Then he went to the University of Wisconsin in 1929, where he had a fellowship. Even after he had received his Ph.D., Hayakawa's race was a handicap. When he couldn't find work as a teacher, he remained at Wisconsin, where he was a teaching assistant, until the university offered him a position as what he calls "a traveling lecturer." Teaching freshman English in rural areas during the cold Wisconsin winters made him more determined than ever to succeed in the academic world. He would often cite this experience as one of the causes of his interest in general semantics, saying his fascination with words grew out of his discovery that his students' English usage differed with the occasion. Later on, he would also say that he went into general semantics because he was concerned with the rise of Nazism, which he attributed to people's failure to see the real intentions of fascist orators and propagandists.

Hayakawa discovered general semantics as such when the University of Wisconsin began an experiment in the teaching of Freshman English. The coordinator of the experiment had devised various approaches to the subject, one of which was semantics. Part of Hayakawa's assignment was preparing a textbook for his class. This project took him to the University of Michigan during the summer of 1938, where he was taking courses in linguistics, but "complaining," as he puts it, "that there were no courses in general semantics. So they asked me to lecture on Korzybski [one of the founders of the discipline] in a lexicography course. I did, although I expected to be lectured to on Korzybski rather than do the lecturing myself, because I knew so little about him." Hayakawa then wrote to Korzybski, who replied by telegram, inviting him to attend "an intensive one-week seminar" in general semantics.

Korzybski was a former officer in the army of the Czar, and he had not lost his old military frame of mind. He found in Hayakawa, a "favorite pupil and disciple." Hayakawa, in turn, thought him "very paternal and kind." At Chicago's Institute of General Semantics, the younger man took possession of his master's brief but important paper and incorporated it into the textbook he was writing for his class at Wisconsin. This was the basis of *Language in Action*, at that time a spiral-bound, mimeographed paper, which Hayakawa immediately had copyrighted. He soon began to send it to different universities, and a number of them, including Syracuse, began to use it as a text.

Hayakawa's race continued to make it difficult for him to find employment as a college teacher. The following year when he was hired at Illinois Institute of Technology, a job he took to be near his master, the process was not simple. "The idea of hiring a Japanese to be an English instructor was too far out," he remembers, "They had to have a full faculty meeting, despite the fact that I already had my Ph.D. and a book out by then. I don't mean *Language in Action*," he explains, "but my scholarly work on Oliver Wendell Holmes. But imagine! A full faculty meeting. To decide on one lousy instructor!"

Soon after Hayakawa moved to Chicago, his Japanese background again became an issue. When he was listed as an enemy alien by the local draft board, he duly went in to argue that he shouldn't be classified as an enemy. "I said to the board members," he recalls, "I can't be an enemy alien because we're not at war with Canada." Telling the story today, still with the youthful enthusiasm of a boy who has done the right thing and knows it, Hayakawa says, "So sure enough, that's right, they reclassified me as 1-A. I never heard another thing from them for years." Actually, he was reclassified as an enemy alien again three years later, but managed to have that classification changed also.

Hayakawa says that "a garbled version" of this story circulates among the New Left. According to it, he disguised himself as a Negro to escape the relocation camps. Recounting the story, he says, "Anyway, when B'nai B'rith honored me as the 'Man of the Year' and the SDS Jewish radical students protested it, they yelled over and over again, 'Where were you dur-

ing World War Two?' " Then he explains that he was writing
for the Chicago *Sun* book section during these years as a regular reviewer and lecturing all over Chicago.

As the demand for *Language in Action* increased, he was
also revising the book for the fourth time during this period
and sending it out to different publishers. He eventually chose
Harcourt, Brace and Company, he says, because they had published some of his favorite authors, like T. S. Eliot and e. e.
cummings. Hayakawa's book was an instant success, "a Book-
of-the-Month Club selection," the semanticist proudly recalls.

Despite his accomplishments, Hayakawa was denied a home
in a white neighborhood and had to live in the Negro section
of Chicago. Perhaps out of a desire to prove his loyalty to the
United States, he had joined the psychological warfare committee for civil defense and gave lectures in the Chicago area. The
war had taken many students out of the Institute, so he was
left with ample time for himself. Income from his successful
book left him free to take several one-week "intensive" courses
in psychoanalysis in Topeka, Kansas, under Menninger. He
also studied sociology and anthropology in such programs,
using the latter work as a basis for a course he taught engineering students at the Institute.

It was at this time, too, that he entered the field of journalism, after accepting an offer to write a column for a Negro
weekly, *The Chicago Defender*. About this venture, Hayakawa
says, "I immediately got into trouble with the authorities at Illinois Institute of Technology because they thought it was very
damaging and dangerous for any of us to be mixed up with a
Negro newspaper, especially for a Japanese." He explains,
"This was during the first few nervous months of the war.
There was even a rumor published in the Hearst newspapers
that Japanese naval officers had been working in the Negro
community to create disloyalty for the United States." He remembers this laughing. Then he sobers. "You know, I was
really threatened with firing if I didn't quit that paper."

Hayakawa says he replied quietly, "Thank you for your advice. I'll think it over." But he also defied his superior, something he had rarely done before. "I never went back to see him," he explains, "and just kept on writing right through 1947."

Hayakawa proudly cites as an example of his continuing pursuit of knowledge during his stay in Illinois the fact that he took evening and summer courses at the Institute of Modern Art under J. Mahoney Naji, "the greatest," he says, in modern art. Discussing this period of his life, the semanticist raises his hands and narrows his eyes, after a long pause saying thoughtfully, "Here you see a pattern developing which is very much me. I got a Ph.D. in English, the conventional literary scholar. I make my reputation in something else altogether, in semantics. From there on I wander off into modern art, into psychology and anthropology. So that's a characteristic form of my life. Suddenly instead of going more deeply into any one subject, I spread out in new directions altogether." Hayakawa also became interested in jazz during this time, and after radio broadcasts, lectures and articles, delved into another area, that of African art.

By the early fifties, he had revised and enlarged his book on general semantics and published it under the new title *Language in Thought and Action.* He was by now well-known to Freshman English teachers, and invitations for paid lectures were increasing. One came from San Francisco State in 1952. Like many other professors, Hayakawa found the location of the college attractive. In 1955, he moved to California.

When he failed to become a dominant figure at the college, he turned to playing a patriarchal role among graduate students. They looked upon Hayakawa with wonder because he had accomplished so much. They were flattered by his casual attitude toward them, and they wished to emulate his career.

Hayakawa now thought of himself as a kind of Messiah. He wanted to spread the message of semantics in order to eradicate many of the problems of mankind. Later he would explain, "It's our fond hope that if there are enough semanticists, fascism will never have a chance, and they won't be able to sell cigarettes, either." Just as he had done twenty years earlier at the University of Michigan, he now began to urge that more courses in semantics be taught at San Francisco State. But now he was a leader in his field. His colleagues, who felt that his claims to expertise in various areas impressed only the ignorant, looked down on him more than ever, especially when he seemed to measure his intellectual achievement by his royalties. "Just last year it sold 60,000 copies," he would say. One professor says in criticism of him, "Hayakawa got an honorary degree from a commercial art institute, and he thinks he's an art critic."

Hayakawa's life was becoming routine. Every semester he taught English 126, which attracted numerous students, some of whom finished the course less enthusiastically than they had begun. One of them, Howard Beckmann, upon hearing the news of Hayakawa's appointment as college president, wrote to the student daily of San Francisco State: "Hayakawa would consider any criticism of him as merely 'statements about the speakers,' his favorite defensive move . . . clumsily defended by his assortment of eclectic, pseudo-intellectual 'analytical tools.'" By now the course in semantics was taught in several sections with TV monitors, and supervised by student assistants. Richard Bratset, who later became professor of world literature at the college, was one of them.

Bratset, who had been fascinated by the professor of general semantics, had decided to go into that field because of his encouragement. In time, Bratset had decided that general semantics was "a fraud." He would say later that it would eventually disappear from the academic world along with Dr. Hayakawa. Bratset sees his old mentor as a promotor of his subject rather than as a scholar. In fact, Hayakawa's contribution to the field consisted only of simplifying Korzybski's complex theories.

By now, Hayakawa had exhausted his liberal interests, fair

housing and civil rights among others. His everyday life seemed to bore him, and he turned more frequently to his students, sometimes pursuing his relationships with them beyond the professional level. To new professors at the college, he seemed extremely polite and cordial. One of them who went out on strike only after long deliberation, was to say: "He was not like some other professors around here. If you met him in the halls, he would nod smilingly, or say hello or something." Over the years, Hayakawa had become more critical of his colleagues who sympathized with the New Left, but they either ignored his criticism or dismissed it with sardonic smiles. He also irritated liberal members of the faculty who did not sympathize with the New Left when he insisted on trying to discuss subjects like the students' right to free speech, which most people already took for granted.

On November 14, the day the San Francisco police revitalized the BSU strike by their random attacks on the students, Hayakawa had gone to see one of his protégés, Barry Goodfield. As they nibbled cheese and sipped wine, Hayakawa expressed his opposition to faculty members who seemed to him to condone everything the blacks at the college did. That night, when he returned home, he wrote what the AFT professors termed his "law and order" speech. Hayakawa says he knew it was an important speech and that he wrote it carefully and arranged to have it mimeographed to ensure adequate coverage by the press. In his speech, Hayakawa condemned the liberal professors on campus for taking what he claimed was a condescending attitude toward the blacks by making fewer demands on them than on whites. When he challenged his colleagues to control violence on campus by forming their own patrols if they opposed the presence of police, he was both cheered and booed. After the speech, he left the auditorium to seek out the press corps, who were eagerly awaiting something different. They gave his speech ample space. What had most irritated those who had booed the semanticist was his tone. As a local reporter put it, Hayakawa gave his colleagues "a lesson in semantics."

Ten days after the story appeared in the papers, Hayakawa was appointed acting president. The trustees shared the administration's view that at the heart of the problem at the college were the liberal faculty members, and Hayakawa had informed the chancellor in notes and by his November 14 statement that he did not support professors who were pro-black.

His brief press release on the afternoon of November 26, when he announced that the college would be closed for the rest of the week, a period which included the Thanksgiving holidays, set the tone of his presidency: he was to solve the problem alone. The consultations with various bodies which his predecessors had so scrupulously held seemed to him only a hindrance. Also, he would be at a disadvantage in working with professional administrators. He was not familiar with the functions of different individuals at the college, and his impulsive orders might conflict with established procedures. Only a few minutes after he made the announcement that the college would be closed, he told top administrators that he would fire all professors who sided with the striking students. Some of the more experienced administrators took his remarks lightly, without commenting. To them, he sounded like an angry little boy revealing his fantasies. But others were alarmed, and said so. One of these administrators pointed out that the new acting president's policies were no different from those of State Superintendent of Public Instruction Max Rafferty who, in the several years he had been a public official, had repeatedly denounced liberals as well as the left.

Hayakawa began his administration by surrounding himself with people who were loyal to him rather than to the institution. He was tired of being talked out of what he felt were good ideas. He had wanted to have music played over a public address system and to have flowers planted all over campus to soothe the angry students. Although these ideas had been rejected, another plan—actually originated by Harvey Yorke—had been put into practice. Hayakawa asked his student supporters to wear blue arm bands. The small group who responded believed that the college's problems could be solved through businessmen's and industrialists' benevolence toward minority groups. The blue arm bands made the students who sympathized with the new acting president an easy target. Two Central Committee members who were driving home from campus one afternoon spotted one of Hayakawa's supporters walking innocently down the street. After stopping their car right in front of the "blue boy," as the acting president's supporters were called, the black students knocked him to the ground and kicked him.

On the evening of November 26, when Hayakawa was beginning a new era at the college, ex-President Robert Smith stepped down from the jet which had brought him from Los Angeles. Confronted by a persistent reporter, he insisted that he had already made a statement to the man's colleague in Los Angeles. When the reporter kept asking what Smith was going to do next, the former president bluntly replied, "I am going to go home now and change my clothes and see my family and have dinner with them."

The following day the campus was deserted. Only a few administrators showed up. With the assistance of his public relations officer, Hayakawa was busy learning what had been going on in the administration during the previous twenty days. Then he devoted himelf to considering the reopening of the college. First the police were contacted and told to handle the crisis as they saw fit, which meant that they would counteract the rebellion by massive force, either by transferring officers from routine, nonemergency duties and having others work overtime, or by calling in those from neighboring cities under a mutual-assistance pact.

While Hayakawa was formulating his policies, the BSU leaders were discussing the new president and their own policy. Except for Jack Alexis, who had attended most of the faculty meetings over the past two weeks, no one knew anything about the new president. When Alexis told the blacks that Hayakawa was a reactionary who would do exactly what the governor and the trustees wanted, or at least nothing of which those authorities would disapprove, what Stokely Carmichael had told the BSU three weeks earlier about power began to make more sense. The appointment of S. I. Hayakawa seemed a perfect example of "real power." The trustees had named a head of the college who would do exactly what they wanted without instructions.

On Saturday, November 30, Hayakawa confirmed their beliefs. At a lengthy and well-publicized press conference held at the Press Club downtown, he reaffirmed the trustees' policy of keeping the campus open. He also gave the black students some advice in the course of his statement, suggesting that they learn how to make demands. He said society was willing to offer much more than the very little the blacks were asking for. No administrator within recent memory had dared to tell the blacks openly what to do. Black students were also angered by Hayakawa's constant references to his ethnic background, particularly when Japanese-American students who sympathized with them told them that Hayakawa had always disassociated himself from the Japanese-American community. To the blacks, Hayakawa seemed an Uncle Tom. He would collaborate with the power structure, the source of their problems, and only occasionally obtain concessions, insignificant ones, at that. He also seemed their "enemy." For him there was no middle ground, as he himself had said. He would fight them with the police, and his rhetoric was devoid of reference to the social and economic causes of their psychology.

That night when the Central Committee met, Jerry Varnado addressed the group without challenge. He classified all administrators and all those who did not side with the blacks in the same category as Hayakawa, and it seemed to those who listened that Varnado had been right all along. Now a new period in the history of the BSU began. As Jack Alexis describes it—"From that time on, we became a military group. All we discussed was military strategy. There would be days, after Hayakawa took over, when as many as fifty black students came to school armed with revolvers just in case the police used their firearms."

9

Law and Order

JUST A FEW MILES WEST OF THE SAN FRANCISCO STATE COLLEGE campus is a man-made lake. It provides a quiet refuge for occasional fishermen, many of whom live nearby in Park-merced, a group of apartments owned by the Metropolitan Life Insurance Company. The silence at Lake Merced is sometimes broken by riflemen who come to practice at the firing range on its western shores.

On Monday morning, December 2, there was unusual bustle around the firing range as police patrol cars and vans brought in officers to assist those already stationed on campus in case trouble erupted. Shortly after seven o'clock, just as the last of the nearly one hundred policemen were arriving, a gray State of California car entered the rifle range. Smiling and arranging his vest, S. I. Hayakawa emerged. He had come to speak to the men on the police force personally, to show his appreciation for what they were doing. After a series of jovial smiles and hand-shakes, the acting president of San Francisco State College be-came earnest. He told the policemen that their main job would be that of public relations because they would be met with hos-tility from students and faculty. Hayakawa explained to the officers that they should try to establish rapport with the students. "Smile at them," the semanticist said. "Let them see you as people and not just as uniforms." Then he went on to tell the policemen not to be upset if the students called them names. "It doesn't really hurt you," he said, "and it has a therapeutic effect on them." Hayakawa then assured the officers that any arrests they made would not be in vain because his administration would not grant amnesty to campus offenders.

He set out to return to his office after this talk. As his car went by the main entrance to the campus, he saw a few professors passing out leaflets, and students talking to them. Inside the administration building, he met secretaries and administrative assistants who had come to work earlier than usual that day, perhaps out of curiosity to see how the first day of school under the new president would go. Hayakawa himself was unsure of what would develop, although he had explained during his press conference that he would be harsher on offenders than his predecessors had been.

Shortly before eight o'clock, as he peered out of his office window, he noticed a handful of his supporters who were handing out blue arm bands and leaflets written by Harvey Yorke, his public relations man. Hayakawa decided to say a few words of encouragement to the students who supported him. Just as he was stepping out of his office, he heard amplified voices from the other side of the building. A white student had parked his truck outside the administration building, where he was using sound equipment to solicit support for the strike. Hayakawa headed toward the sound, angered by this defiance. One of his first actions as president had been to order notices posted all over campus forbidding the use of such equipment. With short, quick steps, he left the building, stopping briefly at the south entrance, where his multi-colored tam-o'-shanter made a bright spot against the glass door. Lips compressed, he walked toward the sound truck, and made his way through the surprised students gathered around it. In a voice quivering with anger, Hayakawa told the speaker that the use of sound equipment was forbidden and that he, as president of the college, ordered him to stop immediately. Somewhat surprised at this interruption, the student stared. Before he could reply, Hayakawa had jumped onto the truck and attempted to grab the microphone out of the student's hands. Failing to do so, he looked around wildly. Then he noticed the wires of the amplifier. He stepped forward and pulled at them until the sound stopped. Seemingly proud of his victory, Hayakawa stood, hands at his waist, feet apart. The striking students had hardly been able to take in what had happened. Not knowing what else to do, they began to chant, "On strike, shut it down." Those who were standing nearest to the truck climbed up, and began to push at Hayakawa.

"Don't shove me! I'm the president," Hayakawa yelled in a high, shrieking voice. "I'm the president!" he repeated.

As he was fighting to stay on the truck, Hayakawa noticed that one of the students who was looking on helplessly was wearing the blue arm band which marked his supporters. The young man's hands were full of arm bands and leaflets he had been offering to students who passed by. Breaking free of those who were shoving him, the acting president reached over and grabbed the leaflets from his supporter. Saying, "Here, take them!" he began to throw the leaflets at the angry students standing around the truck. Because tension was increasing, newsmen who had been watching the scene advised Hayakawa to leave before something happened to him. As he was stepping down from the truck, one of the rebellious students grabbed the president's tam, and started it flying from one hand to another. When the helpless administrator failed to get it back, he began to walk away amid general laughter. Then a young reporter caught his headpiece and returned it to him.

That evening, Hayakawa would be seen on the television screens of California in this single-handed battle with leftist students, and the governor of California, former actor Ronald

Reagan, would say, "I think we have found our man." The new president of the college seemed to be acting out the fantasies of many conservatives who wanted to respond to the radical students' disruptions with physical force, but who would never have made such a public display of themselves. Black students treated the incident with scorn. In the words of Jerry Varnado, "He would never have dared to do that to us, that buffoon. We would have trampled all over him."

Later that morning, professors and students picketed campus buildings and distributed leaflets. Art Bierman, who had organized his dissident colleagues into FORCE, Faculty Organization for Responsibility in College Education, had helped put together an elaborate five-page leaflet. In addition to demanding the removal of both the new acting president and the police, this group was also asking that their working conditions be improved and that the fifty or so professors who were scheduled to be dismissed the following semester be retained at the college.

Around noon, students and faculty began to converge on the Speakers' Platform for a rally. After black student speakers had urged their supporters "to fight the pigs," the group marched on the Administration Building. There, they were met by the police, but without incident they marched on the BSS and later on the Science Building, chanting, breaking windows, and throwing rocks at policemen who formed protective lines before the building under attack. By mid-afternoon, the strikers had dispersed. They returned to campus the following morning, ten of their number having been arrested. Later on in the day, Hayakawa announced the suspension of five students whose names were mentioned in the local newspapers as strike leaders. Among them were Jerry Varnado and John Levin.

On Wednesday, the next day, at nine o'clock, police broke up a picket line of twenty students in front of the BSS Building and disrupted an impromptu skit in which Hayakawa and those who controlled the state of California were being ridiculed. A small crowd took refuge in the cafeteria, thinking the police would not follow. But the officers went after them, knocking down other students who happened to be in the way. The police arrested ten students, hitting some of them passionately.

By noon, most of the strikers had already heard of the morning's events and were talking quietly about the arrests in small groups gathered in the central area of campus for a rally. Community leaders who had participated in the summer talks had come to campus again for the first time since the crisis began on November 6, in order to show their support for the strike. One after another, they stood on the platform, denouncing the police and expressing their support for the strike. Berkeley Councilman Ron Dellums told a cheering crowd: "Principles are not negotiable, not discussable, not compromisable. The only thing we in the black community can say to you is 'Right on, right on!' "

Strike activities ended that day with several students injured and thirty arrested. But there were casualties among the police, too. An officer was knocked unconscious when a brick hurled by a student hit his neck. Others were bloodied. Many students viewed police casualities as meaningful landmarks in the history of higher education in America, saying they could be expected to multiply during the coming days. But the police grew cautious. Unless they outnumbered the students, they made it a policy to avoid such confrontations.

By three o'clock that afternoon, strikers had left a campus eerie and deserted. Tired newsmen were sitting on the floor leaning back against the walls outside the room where Hayakawa was scheduled to make a statement to the press. Just as on the previous day, the new acting president was late. Some of the reporters wandered off to the public information office on the second floor to find out if Harvey Yorke could tell them when his boss would appear. They found Yorke typing. Head straight up, he peered out from under his lenses. He said he could not talk to anyone right now, but that as soon as he had finished the statement he was typing, his boss would meet the press.

Yorke's job had originally consisted of writing dull press releases about events on campus and answering calls from the public, but as turmoil increased at the college he had become more of a press secretary. Now what he wrote no longer ended up in the wastebaskets of city rooms. Yorke's words reached millions of Americans, and he had become an important figure at the college. Under the other two presidents he had served during the past year, he had been told exactly what to say. Only occasionally was he given the opportunity to use his talents. When Summerskill resigned, Yorke had cautiously pointed out that it would be a mistake to let the president's statement of resignation stand as it was written. Summerskill, whose major was clinical psychology, told him to polish it as he pleased. The public relations man was to recall frequently that he had made sense out of the distressed Summerskill's complicated statement.

Under Smith, Yorke still had to follow the president's rough drafts in preparing releases, but with Hayakawa, his function had changed. The new acting president did not wish to be bothered with details. He left it up to Yorke to decide on what the administration's official response to the daily disturbances would be. Hayakawa's attitude toward his new job suited Yorke's concept of how a college should be run. The public relations expert saw no difference between managing a factory and running a college. "Any organization could be subject to this kind of disruption," he would say. "Good executives don't bother with any more detail than they have to."

Yorke, whose father was a public relations man for a motion picture company, had secured a small office at the college and had had it equipped with coffee machines and special telephones for the press. Now he politely directed the impatient newsmen to that room. As soon as he had finished typing his press release, for which he had personally been gathering information all day, he gave it to the secretary to run off on the ditto machine. A few minutes later, he picked up over forty copies of the one-page release and hurried downstairs. When he appeared in front of the president's office, the waiting reporters began to enter the press room, after a campus policeman who stood outside had checked their credentials. Until Hayakawa's presidency, press conferences on campus had been open to students, but Yorke had decided to bar students from the conferences because his boss's reaction to some of their questions might prove embarrassing to the administration.

The press room was decorated with flowers, gifts from the new president's well-wishers. Hayakawa displayed these flowers both to show how much the public loved him and to appear on the television screen in an atmosphere of joy. Just as on the previous day, he insistently maintained that many students had attended classes and that the school had functioned normally. When his answers began to get repetitious, one reporter decided to change the subject by asking how it felt to be the president of a college which was beginning to resemble an armed camp. Hayakawa smiled. "This has been the most exciting day of my life," he explained, "since my tenth birthday, when I rode on a roller coaster for the first time." Reporters who had witnessed bloody fights earlier that day betrayed by their ensuing questions that they considered this comparison inappropriate, but it was evident that Hayakawa meant what he had said. Several weeks later, when he was being interviewed on National Educational Television by Edwin Newman, he interpreted his remark for his audience, saying that the public had misunderstood him. He told Newman that his excitement at riding a roller coaster for the first time was not pleasant, but sickening. Actually, he had not been aware of the bloody incidents on campus that day, just as he was unaware of many other aspects of the strike. He had relied on Yorke's statement, which placed the burden of guilt on the students, and on his own belief that he did not need all the evidence to judge the situation at the college.

Hayakawa's role was becoming clearer. The strike at the college had turned into a criminal matter, which the large numbers of policemen assigned to the campus would take care of, and the acting president appeared to be the major and most colorful apologist for a law-and-order policy toward student turmoil. Now that he was becoming well-known, requests to interview him were increasing. By the middle of the week, he had already granted many interviews.

One of them was witnessed by Professor of Education A. Daniel Peck, who had come to see the new president on business. Due to Hayakawa's overloaded schedule, Peck was to see him at the same time as the Los Angeles *Times* education reporter, John Dreyfuss. When Peck arrived, a reporter from a radio station was asking, off the record, what the president thought of his new job. Without a word, Hayakawa went to the cabinet in his office, brought out a bottle of scotch, and offered a drink to everyone. Finally came the turn of Dreyfuss, who had flown up from Los Angeles to cover the crisis at the college. He seemed surprised to learn that Peck had an appointment with Hayakawa at the same hour. Without hesitation, the semanticist told the two men that he would see them together. Then they found out that a representative from the mayor's office was also to see the new president of the college during that time.

When the confusion had subsided, Dreyfuss said, "I would appreciate it, Dr. Hayakawa, if you would begin by telling me what you think of the situation at the college."

"I can't tell you anything unless you want to know something," quipped Hayakawa. He takes great delight in shocking his listeners, particularly those who don't know him, and often strives to appear free of convention. "I just don't follow everybody's fashion," he once said.

Surprised at getting such a blunt reply, the reporter from Los

Angeles asked a specific question, which Hayakawa quickly referred to Peck. While Peck was answering, the new president raised himself to the edge of his desk. After briefly dangling his unshod feet in the air, he jumped back onto the floor and curled his toes into the plush carpet. Offering his guests another drink, he said pensively, "You know, one thing bad about this job is that I don't get enough exercise." He explained that he had a crick in his neck and that turning somersaults helped it. After taking a quick gulp, the new president began to do jumps. While the amazed reporter tried to continue the interview, Hayakawa went to a corner of the room opposite him, got down on his haunches, and turned a somersault, landing in the middle of the room.

"It's amazing, Dr. Hayakawa, a man of your age in shape to do that," Dreyfuss complimented him. "My six-year-old son would be surprised." As if encouraged by his comments, Hayakawa returned to the corner and repeated his feat.

"It's incredible that you're in such good shape," the reporter said, as the semanticist landed in the middle of the room again.

"Do you really think so?" he asked.

The fact that Hayakawa was now president made the AFT strike almost a certainty. During Smith's presidency, the professors had found it difficult to make such a decision, because they could not lump him with conservative Californians. Colleagues who knew Robert Smith personally could not in all honesty ascribe to him the political policies they attributed to the distant chancellor or trustees. But the new president had made it clear that he did not intend to deviate from the trustees' policies. On the evening of the third school day of Hayakawa's presidency, the union professors voted to request a strike sanction from the Labor Council, the coalition of most of the city's unions. According to this procedure, if the strike were sanctioned, the AFT would be permitted to present its demands to the administration. Then, if the demands were not met, the professors' organization could go out on strike and have their strike honored by other unions. Discouraged, perhaps because this procedure seemed cumbersome to them, professors like William Stanton unsuccessfully tried to talk their colleagues into an immediate walkout.

Mayor Joseph Alioto of San Francisco was alarmed at the AFT's request for a strike sanction, and said that he would try to prevent the professors' getting it. At the time, he was considering running for governor against Ronald Reagan, and he was distressed at seeing his city become the scene of prolonged student unrest. A strike by the teachers would put San Francisco's organized labor force behind the rebellious students. Alioto's past associations with labor might jeopardize his chances of being elected governor if the polls were right about the electorate's vehement opposition to the students. The mayor quickly summoned a nationally known mediator, Charles Haughton, from Washington, and later on set up a citizens committee composed of civic leaders who were to act as an advisory body. Unlike most of those involved in the turmoil at State, Alioto approached the students without rancor. He always showed a willingness to negotiate with them. But some of them claimed that the mayor's open-mindedness only revealed his desperation.

Alioto is a fast-talking, smooth politician, who entered politics at a late age. A native San Franciscan, he was already a successful corporation lawyer who estimated his wealth at some six million dollars when he was elected mayor. He had often expressed his belief in compromise politics. During the strike, he only grinned when questioners brought up the "nonnegotiability" of the black students' demands. Yet he had not been successful in bringing about a solution to the crisis.

The trustees reacted coldly to the idea of mediation. Meriam had said, "The trustees will consider no demands until order is restored on campus," and added that even if order *were* restored, the group would handle events in their own way.

This prompted the AFT to issue an ultimatum that if meaningful negotiations didn't begin by Friday the thirteenth, they would strike with or without sanction.

By the end of Hayakawa's first week as president, conditions at the college had deteriorated, and there was evidence that the following week might be even worse. Encouraged by their successful daily disruptions, the students announced additional support for the days to come. The Academic Senate, dissatisfied with Hayakawa's policy of not involving it in running the college, requested that the new president appear before it "to explain why he's doing what he is doing." In response to pressure, particularly from the mayor, Hayakawa announced, with the chancellor's approval, that San Francisco State would have a Black Studies Department equal to other departments with 11.3 faculty positions.

He revealed these concessions, along with a few others, in a large auditorium located in the Creative Arts Building. Although it was only one hundred yards west of his office in the Administration Building, the new president had gone there in a car escorted by several policemen. A few students were watching as he left the building after making his announcement, leaving through a back door to enter a waiting car. He had walked down the corridor accompanied by four officers, two in front and two behind him. The students booed as he boarded the car, while he smiled and talked cordially to his police escort. When the car drove off, the students began to compare the new acting president to a colonial governor. They said that their college was being run by outsiders who had never been on campus and who had chosen an unpopular member of the local community to rule. The students agreed further that Hayakawa's appointment had not been made through normal channels and that he could maintain his power only through military force.

The new president's second week began with warnings that the dissidents would shut down the college. By now, the main objective of both the white strike supporters and the administration was to determine whether the college was functioning normally. Through statistics furnished by Harvey Yorke, Hayakawa maintained that the college was in operation. Television, radio, and newspaper reporters repeated his contention every day, along with the strikers' contention that the college was not operating normally because of continuous violence and the presence of police on campus.

The black students felt that the strike had achieved its purpose and continued to strike. It was attracting national attention to them. Daily demonstrations and fights and the constant presence of police on campus were gaining new white students as supporters every day. Nesbitt Crutchfield said, "We don't want any more convocations or debates or mediations." Jerry Varnado claimed later, "If Kay Tsenin joined us, called the police 'pigs' and threw rocks at them, then we must have been doing well." Kay Tsenin was a conservative student politician who only a year earlier had joined others with a similar bent to urge that state legislators investigate the BSU.

Every morning, hundreds of students came to school only to participate in the strike. They had already either made alternative arrangements for class attendance with their professors or had dismissed their courses as lost. Now, instead of the relatively dull days they had previously spent on campus, they enjoyed the warmth and excitement of social commitment. A feeling of solidarity usually followed strike activities, and support of a common cause served as an introduction which carried its own recommendation. Many student observers were to comment on the increased sexual activity which accompanied the strike.

The police department soon began to feel it could not afford to keep hundreds of officers at San Francisco State every day. Already the cost of overtime was beginning to make its effects felt in City Hall. Patience on the part of the police was also diminishing, despite the sincere belief of some of the officers that they were saving their country from a foreign conspiracy. By Tuesday, December 10, there were signs of frustration. That day, members of the Tactical Squad invited their civilian friends to assist them. One of them waited in the vicinity of the BSS Building, where he attacked students with a blackjack which he had hidden under his jacket. That day also, police began to arrest students who were participating in peaceful demonstrations and to openly provoke fights. After breaking up picket lines in front of the library, the officers harassed students and created enough resentment to cause a scuffle. When no more than two dozen students fled into the cafeteria, the determined officers followed and began to check identifications.

The student reaction was "We're winning! They're up against the wall, so they're trying to get the leaders." On that day John Levin was led away by several officers amid the frightened cries of girls, as if he had expected to be arrested all along. He had always said that democracy here was only a facade. On the day of Levin's arrest, some one hundred students from Sonoma State College had come to San Francisco State to show their support for the strike. Plans had also been made to bring several hundred Latin American and black high school students to campus on a Third World Community Day which had been set up.

On Friday, December 13, the deadline for the AFT's ultimatum, when no agreement had been reached, Hayakawa announced that the college would be closed for Christmas vacation one week earlier than usual. If the college were shut down, Hayakawa believed, the AFT could not strike, and with time the movement against him might disintegrate. He made this decision after consultation with the chancellor and the governor of California who had sent his executive secretary to San Francisco State to be of assistance to the new acting president.

10

The Strike Is Over

HAYAKAWA MANAGED TO AVERT THE TEACHER'S STRIKE BY closing the college early for Christmas vacation. He hoped to quash it completely by political manoeuvring during the extended holidays.

As for the student strike, the new president expected that after the twenty-five-day vacation, support for the strike would have diminished enough to make normal activities possible when the college opened again. But he was wrong.

The black students found it hard to forget the last "glorious" five weeks at San Francisco State. They didn't want to end up just talking about them for the rest of the semester, what Stokely Carmichael had warned them about. Their strike was already having results in other parts of the country, and many BSU chapters were calling on them for advice. At Brandeis, after BSU emissary Bill Middleton had exhorted students to action, buildings were to be taken over and the activities of the college virtually brought to a standstill. At the University of Wisconsin, Nathan Hare was to advise students to strike, and the National Guard was to be called in to restore order on the troubled campus. Hare had gone to Wisconsin as one of the

BSU's Central Committee, of which the students considered him a member.

As long as they were on vacation, the black students enjoyed themselves at events like a big party on December 16 which celebrated Jack Alexis' birthday. Yet their leaders were tired. Since Hayakawa had become president, members of the Central Committee had been holding meetings for several hours nearly every night, talks on strategy in which they felt they did nothing but convey to each other their concern about massive police intervention. The responsibility of directing the large numbers of people who had come to support them—at times estimated at four thousand—made the black student leaders engage in long discussions from which no clear decisions emerged. As a few of the Central Committee members would acknowledge, some of them were on their own "ego trips."

During vacation, the majority of the Central Committee rejected the proposals of two nationally known mediators, Samuel Jackson, one of their own race, and Charles Haughton. Satisfied with the results of the past few weeks, the students wanted more of the same. A few, like Jack Alexis, wanted to enter into negotiations while they were in a position of strength. But the leading faction was determined to continue the strike. This group prevented Alexis from even setting foot on campus lest he meet the mediators.

Unlike the BSU, the AFT welcomed mediation. But the trustees, through their representatives, agreed only to talk with the teachers, rather than commit themselves to negotiations, saying they wanted to hear what the teachers had to say. Efforts to halt the teachers' strike failed. Gary Hawkins, president of the professors' local, was to announce that the trustees would not negotiate and that the AFT would "be forced to strike on January 6."

When the New Year arrived, it became apparent to the police and the administration that the students had not forgotten the past. They sounded as if they had never been on vacation.

As at the height of the strike during the first two weeks of December, their demands were still non-negotiable.

Police tactics were to change with the reopening of the college. As Hayakawa had said earlier, the administration would "be prepared for all eventualities, but I don't want to show my hand at this time." During Smith's administration, the majority of arrested students had been strike followers rather than leaders. But after Hayakawa allowed the police to take charge, they decided to single out student leaders for arrest, believing that the leaders' revolutionary fervor would subside once they had been arrested and beaten up, and that without leadership the strike would die out. The law enforcement officers did not know that student resentment had been growing against strike leaders who sometimes seemed to be avoiding the prospect of arrest during the daily confrontations with police. Arrests of leaders removed all traces of friction among the striking students and increased feelings of solidarity. Now the police had to devise a new strategy. They decided to arrest students en masse, in a number not exceeding one hundred, hoping to tie up loyal strike supporters with the problems of bail, trial procedures, probation, jail sentences, and any other personal or educational hardships arrest might entail.

On Monday morning, January 6, the college reopened with picket lines at all entrances. The most important area on campus for the strikers was now the Nineteenth Avenue entrance. There, marching slowly along the sidewalk under the watchful eyes of the police, students, their off-campus supporters, and the striking teachers formed a long line, which at the peak time of noon included well over one thousand persons. Except when police charged the line, the marchers' mood was festive. In high good humor, one professor, surrounded by his students, even attempted to conduct a psychology class. As the pickets walked along, talking with each other and exchanging anecdotes, sometimes chanting, picket captains stationed every few dozen yards motioned them to keep up a good pace. The students' voices occasionally became loud and threatening when a nonstriking student, grim-faced or embarrassed, crossed the picket line to go to class. Others who wanted to attend classes chose a less crowded entrance. Every time a streetcar approached the college stop on Nineteenth Avenue, the pickets would turn to see what passengers emerged. When students stepped down from the streetcar without books, student pickets greeted them with cheers and applause. Some of the newcomers smiled modestly and hurriedly took a place on the line. Others walked slowly within the crosswalk from the streetcar stop in the middle of the street, giving the clenched fist salute of the Black Panthers until they reached the picket line.

Although professors had been on the picket lines since early morning, the Labor Council did not grant strike sanction to the AFT until about ten o'clock on that first day after vacation. Many labor leaders disapproved of the professors' sympathy for student troublemakers. They believed, like Hayakawa, that once the student crisis was over the teachers would cease to make demands. Yet sanction had been granted. The strike could no longer be termed simply student mischief.

Picket lines at the college now had the sanction of San Francisco's organized labor force, and students were protected by the AFT's picket signs. Police occasionally broke into the picket lines on the pretext of singling out students for whom they had outstanding warrants, but no major violence ensued. The officers felt justified in harassing the students because, whenever arrests were made, the college president denounced the AFT, accusing them of being unable to control the pickets. But the large numbers of officers assigned to the college every day were frustrated.

Student impatience was also increasing. It was true that picketing interfered with the smooth functioning of the college, even if the administration denied it, but the students on the picket lines had no way of preventing those who wished to attend classes from doing so. Sensing their supporters' mood and perhaps sharing their feelings, the Central Committee of the BSU decided to take charge of activities again after three weeks. They scheduled a rally for January 23, the last week of the fall semester, at which they hoped for an attendance of from three to four thousand.

About noon, as planned, students moved out of the picket lines and marched onto campus with the usual chanting and shaking of fists. Black student leaders soon saw that the turnout was not as large as they had anticipated, but they hoped that other supporters would soon appear. Meanwhile, police observers on top of the Administration Building were alerting their forces stationed on campus and in the surrounding area. The crowd appeared to be about three hundred, just the right size. After moving in on those at its edges and scattering them, the police estimated that there were over a hundred people remaining. By the time the speeches began, the officers had taken up positions nearby, out of the students' view but ready for action. When the unsuspecting students ignored the usual warning to disperse which was broadcast over the loudspeakers, considering it another of Hayakawa's threats, the officers moved in on the crowd in single formation, dividing it and circling the people nearest the Speakers' Platform. Observers on the Administration Building jovially estimated the catch to the press at about one hundred.

The police were hoping to break up the strike by making this large arrest. Although the court calendar was already crowded, the one hundred or so student cases which would be the result of this arrest would not interfere seriously with the functioning of the courts. But when police vehicles moved onto campus that cold windy afternoon and officers arrested each striker individually, those in charge came to see that they had made a mistake. By three o'clock, as the officers began to transport the last of the arrestees to jail, it was learned that over four hundred and fifty people had been arrested, most of whom were expected to ask for jury trials. As the police had anticipated, when it came time to post bail, most of the students had to turn their attention away from the strike.

When the fall semester came to an end and the mid-semester recess began, the Central Committee began to discuss ways of concluding the strike. They continued to talk publicly about escalating the struggle. But instructions to their supporters about sabotaging registration in the middle of February proved futile, and during the first week of March an attempt to bomb one of the campus buildings failed when the bomb exploded, leaving a black student maimed. The Central Committee finally agreed on negotiating after they realized that the AFT professors were going to settle their strike.

The black students first revealed their desire to negotiate to the Citizens Committee, appointed by Mayor Alioto and headed by Bishop Hurley, some of its members being sympathetic to the strike. Talks took place at the home of the Associated Students' attorney Frank Brann, and Hayakawa had appointed a Select Committee to engage in negotiations with the students. Most of the faculty members who participated agreed that the black student delegation, led by Jack Alexis, obtained as many concessions as could possibly have been granted.

But internal disagreements obscured the students' aims. A faction led by Jerry Varnado insisted that amnesty be the single most important price of ending the crisis. To Varnado, the strike demands had always been secondary to the strike process. In order to ensure amnesty, the Central Committee made plans to compromise the acting president. Believing Hayakawa to have a particular weakness for women, the BSU planned to lure him to meet with a black girl at her home where a tape recorder had been hidden. The acting president disappointed the black students by showing up on the night of the meeting accompanied by a woman friend. After the failure of this plan, Alexis began the negotiations.

The West Indian could persuasively interpret the black students' demands and analyze their actions. He was able to talk freely about their insecurities and fears as being the basis of their hostility toward whites. As he had done earlier in the crisis, Alexis compared the Black Studies Department and the black students to a child and its mother. "First the mother nurses the child," he said, "and doesn't let it out to anyone." As the child reaches independence, Alexis explained, it can interact with others. "Now that the black students have established themselves through months of fighting," he said, "and discovered that not all whites are necessarily racist, they have no objection to opening their department to students of all races." Alexis also argued on behalf of the weak Third World groups.

Finally, early in the afternoon of March 20, the minority students and the six-member committee signed an agreement. The power of the committee had never really been clear during the talks, although everyone, including its members, assumed that whatever agreement they made would be binding. But Hayakawa waited to decide whether or not he would sign the agreement, and never did so. Later he would say that it was only a series of recommendations. One year later, the black students were symbolically to burn it.

At the time the agreement was signed, the Black Studies Department had already been established. But because of the unusual circumstances surrounding its inception—some people believed that it had literally been founded with the blood of students—it became in practice much more autonomous than other departments. Its members often refused to answer communications from the acting president, and when inquiries from other institutions were received, the department replied with a brochure denouncing the administration, the trustees and the chancellor. On its cover was a drawing of a black youth bearing a rifle and a book entitled "Black Studies."

The question of rehiring Nathan Hare was resolved when both negotiating groups came to the decision that "the apparent failure to rehire Dr. Hare is irrelevant to the institution of the Black Studies Department." Hare was to withdraw as a candidate for chairmanship of the department after he began to publish a new monthly journal, *The Black Scholar*.

The question of admitting Third World students who could not meet the entrance requirements of the college was settled when it was agreed to "raise the percentage of applicants for whom the college may waive admission requirements from 4 percent to 10 percent." The following semester, all the students brought to San Francisco State by minority groups were admitted. As the more practical administrators had predicted, the total number of students who applied for special admission did not exceed the newly established quota. Most of these special admittees would receive financial assistance administered by an associate director of financial aids, a black. The director whom the BSU wanted fired was to stay, but she was no longer to handle the financial affairs of black students. Autonomy from the trustees, a goal of many students both black and white, was never realized. Instead, the trustees were later to tighten their control over student affairs.

An amnesty clause, in the form of a recommendation to Hayakawa, did no good. None of the charges was dropped.

After the agreement which ended the strike had been signed, Jerry Varnado and Benny Stewart walked to the cafeteria. Only a few students were scattered about the room. As the two black students entered, Stewart grabbed a chair near the door and stood up on it. He announced through cupped hands, "The strike is over." The students in the room sat unmoved. They continued their conversations, seemingly tired and uninterested. Without further explanation, Stewart, an angry expression on his face, stepped down from the chair. Then he and Varnado left the cafeteria as quietly as they had come in.

That afternoon, a Mexican-American girl entered the offices of the student daily with an announcement of strike activities for the following day. She had become a student only that semester, and soon after her arrival at the college had joined the Third World Liberation Front to work for the strike. The few weeks she had spent at San Francisco State had been the most exciting in her life, and as a special admittee she was grateful to the student militants, who she felt had opened the doors of the college for people like her. This freshman girl saw her participation in the strike as an expression of gratitude to all those who had been arrested and beaten by the police. When she was told that the strike was over, she said, "Oh, no," close to tears, and left the room.

The strike which had just ended had lasted 134 school days. After it was settled, there was no further trouble on campus.

11

The Beginning

LATE IN JANUARY OF 1970, IN THE EARLY AFTERNOON OF A cold and windy day, Jack Alexis drove to a high school playground on lower Page Street to meet a friend from San Francisco State. After the strike, Alexis had transferred to Stanford University in nearby Palo Alto to do graduate work in the humanities. His lawyers had only recently got him clear of various charges stemming from the crisis at State, among them that of carrying a concealed weapon, a pistol. Alexis was still active on the BSU Central Committee at the state college, where he also taught a class in the Black Studies Department. Earlier that day, he had talked on the phone with Bernard Stringer, another active member of the BSU, who also taught a class at State. Alexis had unsuccessfully attempted to convince Stringer that the final grade he had given one of the black students in his class should be changed from C to at least a B. Not succeeding, Alexis had come to see Stringer in person.

Huddled in an old army fatigue jacket, Stringer was sitting on a bench at the edge of the playground watching black children in their early teens at play. Heavy-set and short, smiling pleasantly, he came to the playground every weekend to supervise the children's games. Stringer took his job very seriously and often voiced his impatience with those who had a light attitude toward "the movement." In addition to off-campus duties such as supervising or tutoring children, Stringer diligently participated every week in the BSU's newly organized political education, or P.E., sessions, as they were called, at which students discussed selected readings from militant black authors, or talked about recent political events. The older, more experienced blacks analyzed the readings or events from their perspective. Although discussions had been carried on even before the strike began, the Central Committee now structured them more rigidly. These meetings constituted part of the Black Studies curriculum, as did much of the work of the BSU. By now the BSU and the Black Studies Department had become almost synonymous. The attitude of most black student leaders was that time was running short. It had become important to prepare new cadres on campus to replace those students who had already moved on, some of them to take jobs with the city's community organizations.

"All right, cut it out," Stringer yelled to a group of children who were starting to fight. Most of them dispersed, but a few came to him, cunningly explained the quarrel and blamed their playmates. When he didn't show any interest, they resumed their play. Alexis sat down beside Stringer on the bench in front of the cyclone fence.

"Have you turned in your grades yet?" the tall West Indian asked casually, folding his raincoat on his lap.

"I have until Monday," Stringer replied. He stretched his short legs, and then crossed his feet.

"I just can't see how you can give a C to a black student," Alexis said firmly.

With the help of a lawyer, he had just succeeded in preventing the immigration authorities from deporting him. Alexis' sense of racial solidarity was growing, and he now referred more often to "my people," as if he were talking about his family.

"He didn't do any work," Stringer said.

Alexis explained that the student could rewrite his paper. "He's shown that he can do a good job in my class and a bad grade will jeopardize his academic standing," he continued.

"That's beside the point," Stringer interrupted. "The administration doesn't have anything to do with it," he said. "It's my class."

After the strike, the black students had taken complete control of the Black Studies Department. Older, full-time black faculty members had relinquished their authority, rationalizing that the BSU was solely responsible for the department's existence. The black students had made the black studies program almost wholly political, just as Nathan Hare had conceived of it and just as its critics had feared. According to the students, the department's primary, if not its sole function was to prepare political militants. In the first regular semester after the strike was settled, the fall of '69, the BSU pressured black faculty members who opposed them to resign. At first, Hayakawa and his assistant Harvey Yorke merely allowed rumors of this situation to leak out to the press. Once it had been established that problems existed in the Black Studies Department, the president began to make accusations, the most dramatic being that a "reign of terror" was occurring. But he had little or no evidence to support his charges.

Having decided that the president was deliberately provoking them in order to get publicity, the black students ignored his charges and continued their everyday activities in the department. Only after Hayakawa had enlisted the support of a group of local black Presbyterian clergymen did the black students ask their supporters in the community to deny the president's allegations.

Harvey Yorke had written the black clergymen's statement in support of his boss and had prepared eagerly for the ministers' press conference. "I wrote down questions for them, and almost to the last one they were asked," he recalls. After the ministers endorsed Hayakawa's allegations against the black students, a local TV newscaster called the president of the state college, to get his reaction to the ministers' pledge of support.

In disbelief, Hayakawa said, "Isn't that amazing! How many ministers were there? Really? I'll be damned."

Reading from the statement with which the president was already familiar, the reporter asked for his reaction.

"This is so exciting. I'm just trying to take it in," was the response. When the reporter asked Hayakawa for an interview, the president hesitated. "Do I want to gum up their act by getting in on it?" he asked. Then he stopped, apparently to subdue his emotion, "I'm just so damned moved I can hardly talk," he explained.

In just a few weeks "the reign of terror" in the Black Studies Department had been forgotten.

Now the fall '69 semester was finished and the two black teachers sat in the open air, negotiating about the black student's grade, while the children from the low-income housing complex nearby played boisterously. Neither young man was impressed with the other's argument. Alexis soon abandoned his appeal, at least for the time being.

Nodding in the direction of the children, he said, "There are thousands of kids like them. Can you imagine what they'll be doing when they grow up?"

The children who were tutored and supervised at play by BSU members were already imitating the older blacks from the college, particularly in their attitudes toward whites and toward those in positions of authority. It seemed to Alexis that these children would grow up to be more militant than his generation had been. Occasionally he singled out one whose habits of play seemed unusually aggressive.

"Look at that one," he would say with an approving smile.

The two BSU members were now joined by three others who had come to borrow brooms and pails from the playground to clean up their off-campus center, which had suffered considerable damage by fire the previous night. Always anticipating attack, the blacks believed the "pigs" had started the fire.

"The checks are ready," one of the newcomers informed Alexis and Stringer. He was referring to the salaries the BSU teachers at San Francisco State received at the end of each month from the Office of the State Comptroller in Sacramento. At the conclusion of the strike, as the black student leaders had planned, most of the staff positions in the Black Studies Department were filled by students, the same students who by their prolonged strike had made Black Studies a legitimate discipline across the country. Shortly after the agreement between the administration and the black students was signed, black Dean of Undergraduate Studies Joseph White began to receive inquiries from many colleges about the new Black Studies Department. Fearing trouble on their own campuses, administrators were asking how to establish a Department of Black Studies before problems arose. Dean White would say later, "The strike at State legitimized the concept of Black Studies. Now it's a respectable discipline." Even the giant Transamerica Corporation was to offer courses in Black Studies in its mobile university on a luxury liner, which sails around the world while classes are being conducted. Although many administrators had been quick to give their black students a variant of a Black Studies Department before trouble erupted, at the University of California in Berkeley a strike modeled on the one at San Francisco State forced the administration to start a School of Ethnic Studies. Also advised by San Francisco State strike leaders, students at the University of Colorado precipitated a crisis over the issue of black studies. As Stokely Carmichael had predicted, the example of the black students at San Francisco State had been followed all over the nation.

As the black students brought out the cleaning equipment

they had come to the playground for, one of them asked Alexis and Stringer if they were planning to go to Bruno the following day. He was referring to the County Jail in San Bruno, where Jerry Varnado was serving a one-year sentence in punishment for his activities at San Francisco State. Varnado was one of the almost seven hundred students from the college who had been arrested during the crisis. Although he felt that he had "made a deal" with the authorities at his trial by pleading guilty to some of the charges against him, so that the others would be dropped, he had been given a sentence of one year, beginning on New Year's Day. The most serious charge against Varnado, the basis of his severe sentence, was that of throwing a fire bomb into the Administration Building during the first week of Hayakawa's acting presidency. He was also charged with inciting to riot.

Like other black students from the college, Alexis had gone to visit Varnado in jail the previous weekend and planned to go again the next day, which was Sunday. During his visits, Varnado had complained about the way the guards were treating him. He had been put into solitary confinement without apparent reason and he was also being denied the medical care his doctor had ordered. Alexis had reassured Varnado that black community leaders, including assemblyman Willie Brown, Varnado's own lawyer, were doing their best to see that he got out of jail and into the hospital. Just recently George Murray had been released from jail, after serving only six months. Murray had assured the judge that he had now reformed. He said he was no longer a member of the Black Panther Party and that he would not participate in the activities of militant students. Murray also said that, while in jail, he had had a religious vision.

While visiting his friend, Alexis had seen other San Francisco State students who were serving time in jail for their strike activities. Most of them were either members of the Progressive Labor Party or those who aspired to membership. These radical students had chosen to defend themselves rather than secure the services of a lawyer, and they usually did not contest the charges against them. Most of them agreed that they had indeed disturbed the peace. Instead of basing their arguments on legal technicalities, such as whether it was legal to give an announcement to disperse over a loudspeaker, they chose to fight over the issues, arguing that there was good cause for their illegal actions. As the radical students expected, they were all found guilty. They accepted their sentences without appealing to a higher court, believing that their stay in jail would provide opportunity to educate their fellow inmates.

The majority of the arrested students had fought the charges against them through their attorneys. Many had been found innocent, and others had received only light sentences. Although student trials had been held all during summer and fall, there were still some to be tried as late as April, 1970. Many students were either put on probation or given suspended sentences, with conditions which forbade their attending rallies or taking part in marches. As a consequence, open opposition to the administration of the college was considerably weakened in the fall of '69, particularly since some twenty-five professors—including young Anton—were fired. But many of the students rationalized that they, too, had harmed their "enemy." Besides property damage on campus, not exceeding $35,000, the strike had cost well over half a million dollars in police overtime. Strike trials had left a backlog of cases in the municipal courts extending well over two years. Another gain the white strikers counted for their side was the radicalization of thousands of people. As a professor of philosophy put it, "In the short run Hayakawa won. But in the long run, we won. Many of the students who gradually came to see the radical viewpoint and eventually lent their support are going to become teachers in this state."

Most of the black students were unimpressed by these gains. They wanted to carry on the work of building up the Department of Black Studies and using it to their own advantage. Alexis was one of them. Stringer shared his view, but he was determined to be more strict than Alexis in preparing the future leaders of the black community.

The two had finally taken shelter from the cold wind in the storage room of the playground, where they began to play dominoes. Now they were talking about President Hayakawa and his political future. At that time, there was considerable speculation that he would take advantage of the publicity he had gotten during and after the strike, and enter politics.

"I'll never forgive myself if that man is elected," Alexis said worriedly, placing a domino. "We brought him into the public eye."

Stringer concentrated on Alexis' move, unimpressed by his friend's concern. "You seem to be doing very well," he said.

The possibility of Hayakawa's being elected to office did not interest Stringer. He thought that the semanticist would be no worse than any other politician.

The acting president, who would eventually be appointed permanent president, did not run for office, after a private poll ordered by the mayor of the city showed that neither the mayor nor Hayakawa could win in the elections of fall, 1970. But Hayakawa had already achieved much more than he had ever hoped for. He would say later, "Why should I run for public office? I am already popular and loved by many people, and I have everything I want. I don't need to run for public office."

Unlike most of the other black students, Alexis frequently analyzed past events. He felt that the BSU's overly aggressive attitudes had caused Robert Smith to resign. Had Smith stayed in office, Alexis thought, the blacks at San Francisco State would have gone much further toward achieving their long-range goals. But others thought that a believer in democratic principles like Smith would never have strengthened the radicals' ranks. As Harold Taylor, the former president of Sarah Lawrence, said, "Had President Smith been given the opportunity to solve the problem in the way he saw fit, the crisis would have been over in a few days."

Alexis had already lost his second domino game. He had also given up hope of convincing Stringer that the black student's grade should be changed. The student would just have to get a C. Leaving the playground to go to an appointment with Varnado's lawyer, the West Indian explained, "I'm going to find out what's happening about Jerry being transferred to the hospital."

Stringer nodded. "Right on," he said.

During the spring semester, 1970, the students continued to run the Black Studies Department. The administration occasionally threatened to withhold their paychecks in objection to what they were doing. Finally, at the end of the semester, those in authority at the college had all the Black Studies teachers fired. In turn, the students moved the department off campus. The administration then formed a committee of black professors from different departments of the college to hire an acceptable black faculty who would form a more conventional Black Studies Department.

Most of those who had led the strike were no longer on campus. Alexis, who had lost his battle with the Department of Justice, had to leave the United States in August of 1970. Varnado had completed his jail sentence in a San Francisco hospital by the time school reopened in the fall. He, like Stewart, went on to law school.

Some people said it really didn't matter whether or not the new department was ever formed. As one administrator put it, "Black Studies was never the issue anyhow."